Stop chasing START ATTRACTING

Discover The Three Pillars That Will Help You Become An Energetic Match To Money, So You Can Do Less And Attract More.

KRISTEN NOELLE

The author of this book does not dispense medical advice or prescribe the use of any technique as a form of treatment for physical, emotional, or medical problems without the advice of a physician, either directly or indirectly. The intent of the author is only to offer information of a general nature to help you in your quest for emotional, physical, and spiritual well-being. In the event you use any of the information in this book for yourself, the author and the publisher assume no responsibility for your actions.

ISBN: 978-1-7348821-0-0

www.kristennoelle.co

DOWNLOAD THE AUDIOBOOK FREE!

Just to say thanks for buying my book, I would like to give you the Audiobook version 100% FREE!

TO DOWNLOAD GO TO:

https://kristennoelle.co/audiobook

For, Mya.

Dearest Mya,

You are the reason why I am doing what I have set forth to do.

Hi hun, this is your mother; I have yet to meet you, yet to know you and yet to hold you in my arms but I felt drawn to write you a letter. I'm not even pregnant with you yet, but I know that at this day and at this time, this letter was meant to be written and that you will exist someday in my lifetime.

So here It goes, and I'll begin with this:

I truly believe from the very depths of my soul that every single one of us is put onto this earth for a greater purpose. You included. And it is this purpose of mine that has led me to write you this exact love letter.

First of all, I love you. And because I love you so, so much, I want you to know that you are capable and powerful beyond measure.

Not too long ago, a friend of mine asked me WHY I decided to go after my dreams of becoming an author. I told him that the reason is because if I were to ever have a daughter, I would want her to know that she can be and do anything she wants to be, and I knew from the bottom of my heart, that I couldn't bear to look you in the eyes and tell you that – unless I followed my own advice and lead by example.

So, this book I wrote is my open love letter for you to see that ***it is possible for you to be whoever you want to be.***

Regardless of what it is!

Baby, do you want to be a dancer? An astronaut? A

doctor? A writer? Perhaps like mum right now, building your own online empire? Anything you want to be, you will be successful in it, as long as you follow your heart and let love be your guide. Do what makes you ultimately happy and fulfilled. You only have ONE life to live, make it count my love.

Will your journey be filled with only rainbows and sunshine? Many times, it will. I say, relish in those moments and celebrate those moments with people who will celebrate and rejoice in your success with you. Those are the people you want to keep in your life.

And as much as I want to take away all the immense heartbreaks and failures you'll go through, I know that you'll probably go through them anyway – more times than you would probably want to.

Girl, you will experience heartbreak, and you will experience failure, but let me be the first to tell you that ***life is always happening FOR you*** – even during the darkest of darkest moments. The only time you have truly failed is if you lost complete hope; and trust me when I say I will NOT let you lose hope in yourself. You my love, have a unique gift to share with the world and you must always remember that and SHARE IT. Don't hide your gifts, baby. Why else do you think you were put on this earth for, silly goose?

Mistakes? Make them. In fact, make plenty of them. Dive into your pool of mistakes and get messy. Mom has made plenty of mistakes, so yes, you are definitely allowed to make them, too. I don't expect you to be perfect my love; really, I don't. But never, EVER let your mistakes define you and remember to OWN them. You are not a victim; in fact, you are the creator of your life. Pick up a pen and write what you wish. Anyone that ever tells you they haven't made a single mistake is not looking out for your best interest. And if it's going to take you many tries to figure it out, SO BE IT. Your life is not a race, nor is it a competition.

Sweet girl, if you are anything like me, you may struggle with a few things that I want you to ALWAYS keep in mind…

Hun, I hate to break it to you, but people will judge, and hate you. I spent a large chunk of my time being controlled by these people. I truly wanted to please everyone (an impossible feat) and it has cost me my sanity, my energy and my precious time. Your haters are going to hate. That is their JOB. Let them do their job and let them be. Everyone is your mirror and you are theirs. Whatever it is that they dislike about you, is only a reflection of what they want and dislike about themselves.

Focus on you, your greater purpose, what you were put on this earth to do, and STAY IN YOUR LANE.

The only person and thing you can control in your entire life is and will only be yourself and your thoughts. I have tried to control people and situations to turn out exactly the way I wanted them to be and that has never worked out for me. In fact, it has only caused me more heartbreak and heavier burdens. Remember baby, that when things are not working out in your favor, pray for things to work out for its higher good. That my love, will give you inner peace.

Finally, I advise you to be good friends with Fear. At first glance, Fear may seem to be scary to be around, and she might make you want to run the other direction but TRUST ME, when I say the farther you run, she will always show up in your life – whether it's now or later. You might as well be well-acquainted with her. Hang out with Fear every single day and make yourself comfortable with her. Your mum has made the mistake of letting Fear control and paralyze her. And as much as I wish Fear would just leave me and you alone, it is part of her job to be a part of our lives. And since we can't choose for her to leave us, I say our best bet is to just accept her. Life will go much, MUCH easier that way.

Mya, wherever you may be when you are reading this letter, even if it so happens that I am sitting right next to you, remember that you are capable and powerful beyond measure. Whatever it is that you want to be and do, **YOU CAN DO IT.** Mom believes in you. You have great gifts that are meant to be shared. Don't hide them from the world.

Loving you always with all my heart and every breath,

Mom

CONTENTS

WHO THIS BOOK IS FOR

If making money feels hard, but you know deep down in the very depths of your soul that you want more abundance and ease in your life, then this book was written for you...

If you were to ask yourself honestly how you feel around money and the answer is one of lack, fear, and scarcity, then this book was designed for you...

If looking at your bank account makes you feel like you've just contracted a disease and you don't know how you'll survive it, then this book is perfect for you...

If you're sitting at your desk wondering what magic pill everyone else swallowed for them to be living the lifestyle they created, and you're still unsure whether it would happen for you, then this book will be your shoulder to lean on...

If you know with every ounce in your being that you were put on this earth to create change, share your gifts, and to leave a legacy, but you're currently held back by your fears, then this book is the light that will guide you...

And finally, if you're ready to stop chasing money (cause my mama once told me, "whatever you chase will run away,") and step into becoming a money magnet, then this book is my gift to you...

I'll see you inside.

How does one become a butterfly? You must want to fly so much that you are willing to give up being a caterpillar.

\- Trina Paulus

INTRODUCTION

Money, money, money.

When you see the word money typed out three times on this page, what are your initial thoughts?

For the longest time, I saw money as stress. If money was a person, I would name it Stress.

Stress would come visit my family each night when the phone rang during dinner and my dad would pick up and angrily have a conversation with it.

Stress would hang out with me while I took a shower in the evening, reminding me that my time was up after five minutes.

Stress would be in my bank account every time I looked at it to pay the bills.

The problem that we face today in our world is the amount of fear and lack that consumes us. We think that there aren't enough resources to go around and so we hoard. We believe that money is limited and so we save and never spend. Money is something we need to have in order to survive, but we have no idea how to attract more of it. The problem is that too many of us are placing money on a pedestal and thinking that it's above us and we aren't worthy of it, when really the real problem is us.

I want you to ask yourself honestly, are you happy with the results in your life right now? Are you happy with the amount of money in your bank account? If the answer is no, then you probably already know you must be doing something wrong. But have you considered that maybe your current beliefs about your life are not helping you get the results you want?

Perhaps those beliefs that you have, have gotten you to where you are right now. But in order for you to get to that next level of success, it's time to try on new beliefs.

I found myself caught between a rock and a hard place when I joined my first multi-level marketing company in 2012. The reason for my dilemma was that even though I firmly believed in the mission of the company that I was a part of, which was something along the lines of helping people heal their illnesses in a natural way, I also equally firmly believed that the act of selling was an evil doing – one that only bad and selfish people participated in. And if I were to stay at this company, I'd have to sell their products!

Seeing the way my dad interacted with salespeople as a small child was enough proof to me that if I were to become one, I would be raising my hand to the devil, let alone volunteering myself to a lifetime of disapproval from my father.

When you are caught between a rock and a hard place and in my case, one of two conflicting beliefs, you must choose one belief (aka path). It's not like you can just walk two paths at the same time. You can try to put one foot on either side of the road, because if you're trying to be in two places at once, pretty soon, you'll end up doing the splits. But guess what? You can't move forward when you're sitting on the ground doing the splits.

So, during that time of my life, while I was at this crossroads, I chose to walk the path that was familiar to me –

one that my parents and ancestors have ingrained in me ever since I was a womb in my mama's belly. I chose to believe that money was a stressor in my life and the root of all evil.

Fast forward five years when I discovered this thing called life coaching. What I realized with this profession was that I could make a living helping people mend their lives. Honestly, I felt like I hit the jackpot. It wasn't until I quickly realized that I'd have to sell myself in order for me to work with clients that I realized I was walking down the wrong path of belief. There was no way I would survive as a life coach if I didn't rebuild my relationship with money. You see, I know firsthand what it's like to "chase money." When you don't have enough of something and you know you need it, you can't help but want to chase it. After all, it's a means of survival.

I also know what it's like to be presented with one's dreams and aspirations but feeling as if it's near impossible to make a living out of it, let alone some extra cash.

If feelings of jealousy creep up whenever you see someone you admire achieve the things you want to achieve, know that you are not alone. I have once felt those feelings as well.

And if the number in your bank account makes you want to crawl up in a ball so that you'll never ever have to come to terms with it, I've been there too.

Now, I'd like to ask you a question...

What does freedom and abundance mean to you? To me, it means being on a secluded island somewhere in Thailand, finding out that same day, that money was flowing into my bank account without me having to trade my time for money.

It honestly took me years to feel the feelings of true abundance and wealth, but once those results came, I knew that I needed to help more people see that the conditions that were placed on them by society may not necessarily be truth.

My intention with this book is to give you the tools to experience the same level of abundance I have felt many times over through practicing the steps I'll be sharing with you in these pages. Just so you know ahead of time, the tools I'll be sharing with you are not at all typical and it requires an open mind and a new way of looking at life.

If the results in your life are not matching up to how you envision your life be at this point, most likely, it has nothing to do with your actions. Your actions only follow your beliefs. So, if you've been using the same beliefs for X amount of years and expect it to help you get to the next level of success you desire, it's almost a requirement to change those beliefs.

This book is divided into three pillars that have been pulled from the system that I created called The Cash Flow Trinity™. This is the same framework that I take my personal clients through so that they become better aligned with abundance and become an energetic match to money.

Pillar 1: Your Money Mission

In order to attract money into your life, you need to first understand what it really is, how it works, and how you can align with it. I don't care how talented you are, you still need to know the rules and mechanics of the game. In this aspect, we are referring to this game called Life. We are all living in this place called earth. It's time to understand how the Universe works so we can work with it instead of against it. Instead of trying to merely survive, I'm all about thriving.

And in order to thrive one must get ahead of the game. I once asked a friend who dropped out of college to start his own business what was the secret to his success despite his reputation in high school of being lazy. He said, "Kristen, I am still lazy. I just find smarter ways to do the same thing. Why use a shovel when there are bulldozers." Pillar One is all about understanding the rules of the game. On top of that, I truly believe that it is our deepest mission to understand how money and abundance works so that we can do great things with money and having it continue to circulate in our world. You were placed on this Earth for a reason – it's time to live out your potential by understanding money and finally use it as the tool as it is, and have it work for you.

Pillar 2: Your Money Mindset

Ever wonder why we are all given 24 hours in a day but some people can achieve more than others? Perhaps they are super human. Or have you ever considered why some people can hit rock bottom and despite their circumstances, they are able to bounce back and sometimes even surpass and go further than where they started? It's all a matter of the way one thinks. Section Two is all about mastering your money mindset. Our minds are free tools that were given to us at birth. Are we taking advantage of it, or are we letting it take control of us? Remember that at the end of the day, your mind is not you, which is why we call it "our minds". Mastering our money mindset means the ability to live your best financial life now. Not tomorrow, or next year, but now at this very moment. The truth is, you are already abundant now. You may not immediately see it, but by the end of this book you'll see how everything has been right in front of you and it's all about shifting your mindset. After all, success is 80% mindset and 20% mechanics.

Pillar 3: Your Financial Environment

Is your environment serving you or is it slowly destroying you? Your environment includes everything that's outside of you – your home, your inner circle, your neighborhood, where you work, even down to the food that you eat is considered your environment. This section is all about creating your environment so that money flows much more easily to you as opposed to the latter. As someone who has grown up in a Feng Shui household and have watched my mom design our home each year to match the energy of the given year, I have witnessed firsthand how energy resides in everything, including this book that you are reading. Learn to work with the energy in your environment instead of having to do all the work yourself. I'm a strong believer that your environment is stronger than will power.

I first had the idea of writing this book after getting off a call with one of my clients and feeling defeated.

Defeated, because I could see in HD how much she was standing in her own way of success and as much as I wanted to go into her home each day and shake her up, I couldn't. It wasn't because she was doing the wrong things. It had nothing to do with that. Her intentions were pure – she wanted success, but the things that were stopping her were not physically visible. In fact, it was all in her mind.

It was then that I realized that it wasn't just her that had the same issue. I came across this same road bump many times over in my life and it required me to first get into alignment, change my level of thinking and situate myself in a nurturing environment in order to get a different set of results.

It pained me to see so many people thinking that

what they need is another action plan or strategy. Those things are absolutely necessary and key to accomplish what you have set forth to do, but if your mindset, environment and alignment is not in place, you'll be running amuck.

Success is 80% mindset and 20% mechanics.

A few days later, I went hiking with my dogs and started thinking about my clients again. I started questioning how I could better serve them so that all of them could get the results that they wanted in their life and business. The thought of a book popped up in my mind and right when that happened, I saw a rather large, orange butterfly hovering and flapping its wings right in front of me. For that brief moment, I was in shock that I was inches away from a butterfly and it didn't fly away. I extended my arm to it and surprisingly the butterfly landed on my right wrist.

In Chinese Metaphysics, there is a term called Evidential Occurrence. It's basically when the Universe is speaking to you or trying to tell you the crazy idea you have in your mind is a good move. Ever ask the Universe for a sign? And then you actually got it? That's evidential occurrence. The truth is that the Universe is always trying to communicate with you. In fact, you are uniquely and divinely guided. The problem is that most people are so wrapped up in their day to day lives, drama, and problems that they aren't paying attention.

I invite you to co-create with the Universe using this book as a tool. In fact, I intentionally placed butterflies throughout this very book to remind you that the world you live in is abundant. So, be on the lookout for them and EXPECT butterflies!

If a candle doesn't lose its flame by giving light to another, then rest assured that there will always be enough for you. The lack you might feel temporarily is made up in your mind. Luckily, we can always change our minds.

Now remember, every time you see a butterfly, it's a reminder to take a moment to feel abundant because you are already abundant. If this sounds like a tricky idea to you, the flaw is in your understanding of reality, not in reality itself. (Don't worry – read the book and you'll know what I mean.)

My suggestion for reading this book is to be open to the contents that I'll be explaining in each chapter. It might not make sense to you the first time around – read the book once more if you have to. Just remember that if you are not getting the results that you want in your life, it's not a matter of doing more, but by changing your level of thinking so that you get different results. You are in the right place at the right time.

I'll join you inside.

Pillar One:

YOUR MONEY MISSION

chapter one:

IS MONEY WHAT WE THINK IT IS?

Nothing in life is to be feared. It is only to be understood.

- Marie Curie

I once had a profound epiphany about money at a vegan Thai restaurant. My partner and I were having lunch one random Tuesday afternoon, and we must have been talking about the subject of money in some way, shape or form, because while I was dipping my veggie spring roll into some bomb homemade dipping sauce, the following words fell out of my partner's mouth:

"Yeah babe, didn't you know only 8% of the world's money exists in physical form."

I'm chewing on my veggie spring roll looking at him, still processing what kind of a bizarre sentence he just spat out at me and decided to question further.

"Wait, what do you mean?"

He then does this thing where he goes into his techno-babble loan officer lingo, and starts spewing out numbers and percentages to me and I start zoning out.

"Only 8% of the world's money exists in physical form?!"

I reach for my phone, while my partner's still speaking in his own language, hoping that my trusty BFF, Google, would say it in a way that makes more sense to me, when my partner suddenly realizes I'm not paying any attention to him and says:

"Okay, pretend that you have $100 in your bank account. Technically, only $8 of it, the bank actually has. That's also why if everyone in the entire world were to run to the bank and take out their money, it wouldn't be even possible."

Now, before you start going into panic mode and run to your nearest bank to pull out all the money you have in your checking account, like they did in the Great Depression; I'd advise for you to read till the end of this book because I'm hoping if I wrote this at all correctly, you'll get your own set of epiphanies.

Basically, what I gathered from our conversation that Tuesday afternoon is that all money is, are numbers on a screen combined with our unwavering faith.

Money is all about faith rather than value.

All this is to say is that money isn't what you think it is. But let's not jump into any assumptions. Let's dive into what you may think or believe money is for you.

What do you think money is? If you had a religious upbringing, you may have been taught things like "money is the root of all evil." Or, that the "love of money is the root of all evil."

And although it isn't the point to denigrate religious beliefs, can you see how your belief about what money is can have a dramatic influence on how you view it? And what do you think it is?

There is probably no other word in the English language that can cause us more grief or joy than the subject of money.

The point is that most of us have been heavily influenced by our parents, society, our friends, or even our religion regarding money, and even which ways are right or wrong on how to make money. For example, sales is one of the most lucrative careers there are, and yet many people are very biased against it.

In a way, it's really a shame that so many people stress out about money. If you were to talk to most people on planet earth, and you asked them what their number one main concern was, money would definitely be in the top three issues. It's something that most of us either don't have enough of, are constantly struggling for, or something that we have an abundance of. There's not much in between! And in later chapters you'll learn why there is no such thing as in between.

But by understanding what money really is, and by learning new tools and techniques, which you will learn in this book, your view of money can turn from stress, to excitement – from worry, to contentment – from scarcity, to abundance.

We live in a world where money affects every single aspect of our lives, and the lives of our loved ones. It can cause more heartache and pain, or more excitement and joy than probably any other single thing there is!

Since money impacts us on so many different levels, it's a really good idea to fully understand what it is.

Let's cover that next...

What is Money?

Before we get into that concept too deeply, consider that the value of money is really something that human beings create. In other words, when you look at a one-hundred-dollar bill, its intrinsic value is not worth much at all – in other words, the actual value of the paper is nearly worthless. Think about it for a moment - the only difference between a one-dollar bill and a one-hundred-dollar bill is the number on it. The paper itself isn't worth hardly anything.

Without purpose, money is just paper.

In a way, money is stored energy. In other words, when you go to work, the energy that you put into your work is exchanged for a dollar amount. That dollar amount represents the amount of energy that you gave to your job – either through actual physical work, or mental work...

But that's the old paradigm way of thinking about money! Today, through the internet, through social media, and through online marketing, it is easier than ever to leverage the power of your time and energy. Instead of trading your time for money, which is a one to one relationship, you can do the work once in a digital format and sell it to millions of people online – which is a one to many relationship – that's much more lucrative...

There are many other options nowadays where you can make money in real estate, the stock market, and even things like bitcoin and other types of currency. Of course, you should do your homework and be very aware of the risks, but if you know what you're doing, you can make a fortune. For example, if you paid just 39 cents in 2010 for one bitcoin, it would be worth over $6,000 today!

The point is that there has never been a better time in human history for the average person like you and me to attract and make money. The first step is to fully understand what it is. The next step is to learn how to align yourself with it – and that's what this book is about...

But money isn't just energy in that very physical, external aspect. At a much deeper level, it's another form of energy, vibration and frequency...

Let me explain...

As you will learn in this book, everything is vibration – everything. Your desk, your car, your house, your body, your brain and even your thoughts are all energy – and everything vibrates at different frequencies.

It was Nikola Tesla who said, "If you want to find the secrets of the universe, think in terms of energy, frequency and vibration." Science, in particular, quantum physics, now proves that everything is vibration – we will discuss this in more detail later.

Basically, at the deepest level, just like everything else, money is vibration. And as Einstein said, everything is energy. If that's the case, then money is energy and, like everything else, it has a certain vibrational frequency. The key or the trick is to understand how the Universe works so that you can become a vibrational match to money...

Lots of money! And maybe more money than you can even imagine right now...

But before we get into the deeper aspects of money, consider the question, why do we even use it? Why do we use money?

A Form of Exchange

The whole reason that humans created money was out of a need for convenience. When you consider how long humans have been on earth, money hasn't really been used for that long. Not long ago, humans would trade feathers for beads, and corn for meat. Can you imagine how inconvenient it would be to have to carry around your corn or meat with you everywhere you went in order to exchange it with others?

So, instead of having to carry around your feathers, your beads, your corn or your meat, instead, you could carry around the money that had an agreed upon value. You could exchange what you had for the value of money, and then use that money to buy whatever you needed. Money is really just a form of exchange – a way to exchange agreed upon value.

But is there anything else about the history of money that may help us to understand it more, so that we can attract more of it into our lives?

Let's dive into that next...

History of Money

The history of money dates back thousands of years, but our paper money got its start back in medieval England, around 1,000 A.D. Before paper money, goldsmiths, money changers, and the public were using gold as currency, or money. But the problem was that gold was risky to store at your home. If you can imagine living back then, it was a little more barbaric than today! Home robberies were much more common back then...

The solution was that people would take their gold to goldsmiths who would store their gold for them, and give them a receipt, otherwise known as a "note" for their gold.

But what happened was that the public soon realized that it was much easier to exchange their paper receipts or notes of gold with each other than it was to go back to the goldsmith, get their gold out of storage, and then pay someone with it...

That is how paper money was created. People started to exchange their "receipts" or "notes" amongst themselves. What the goldsmiths and the bankers realized was that people would hardly ever come to take out their gold, so they started creating more notes than they had worth of gold. This practice by bankers continues to this day, and the system even allows banks to create money out of thin air. That is why the dollar devalues so quickly.

During the birth of America, it was the largest personal financier of the American Revolution Oliver Pollock who created the dollar sign. He did so by using "ps" as an abbreviation for the Spanish pesos in all of his accounting of money with congress. But because his hand writing squished the letters "ps" together, it looked like a "$." His writing is the earliest recorded history of the dollar sign...

So, now that you have a very quick and brief explanation for the history of money, let's discuss what money really is for you and me...

What is Money Now?

I want you to imagine right now that you have an absolute abundance of money. So much money that you wouldn't even be able to spend it all in a life time. If you need an amount, imagine having several billion dollars...

How would that make you feel? How would you feel if suddenly you won the lottery and it was for 5 billion dollars?

Really imagine it for a second!

Would you feel ecstatic? You should! Would you feel

beyond excited? Of course. Would you feel relief? More than likely. Would you feel secure now for the rest of your life? Absolutely, right?

It's a great thing to envision because it can help you to open up the doors of prosperity to you from a vibrational perspective, which we will cover later.

But can you think of any other ways to describe it? How money would make you ***feel***?

How about free? Freedom? And how about suddenly having the ability to experience SO many more new things in life?

The world would be your oyster! You could go anywhere, do anything, and have many new experiences that you are probably not even aware are possible right now...

The two main things you would experience are freedom and new experiences in life. When you think of it from this perspective, when you ask the question, what is money now, the answer could be, money is freedom. Money is security. Money equals new experiences. Money is the feeling of security. Money is the feeling of empowerment. Money is the feeling of excitement and passion, possibility and wonder...

It's really important to understand that your feelings towards money is key to your ability to attract it. You see, via the Law of Attraction, you create your own reality. Most of us have it all backwards as to how to attract money. Most of us think that we won't be happy, feel free, feel secure, feel empowered, feel excited, or passionate UNTIL we have the money...

But that's exactly the opposite of how we create anything in life, and that is usually the main reason why so many struggle to attract money...

In other words, if you want to attract money into your life, you have to feel the feeling of what it would be like to have the money BEFORE you have it – not after.

Hardly any of us are ever taught that this is how it works. Most of us worry and stress out about money which only repels it from us, rather than attracts it to us.

Stop Putting Money on a Pedestal

Have you ever wanted something "so bad" that you felt like you were going to go nuts if you didn't get it? But then when it didn't come, you gave up? But then because you gave up, it suddenly came?

It's not that the Universe wants to play dirty tricks on you! It's simpler than that. It's simply how the Law of Attraction works.

When you want something "so bad," you emit a needy vibration – a frequency of lack instead of a frequency and feeling of abundance, trust, contentment and expectation. And this is what happens when you put money on a pedestal.

When you make money such a major concern in your life, you can't help but to attach a stressed out, worried frequency or vibration to the feeling that you have about money. This is why it's very important to stop putting money on a pedestal...

How should you feel about money instead?

See it as an equal to you. See yourself as deserving to have as much money as you want. See yourself as being worthy of as much money as you want to have.

Most of us have a feeling that we aren't worthy of the good things in life, including money. Not feeling worthy is probably the biggest problem that most of us have. But when you realize that you and everyone else was born worthy regardless of what or what you haven't accomplished in life, then you can be a vibrational match to abundance – and to plenty of money.

In summary:

- Society creates the value of money, not the money itself.
- Money is nothing but energy.
- There has never been a better time in history to become wealthy.

- In order to attract money, you must feel ***FIRST*** the way you'd feel if you had it.
- You must feel worthy of money in order to attract it.

Your money mission:

Be on the look-out for $100 bill money butterflies throughout the book. Every time you see a money butterfly, I want you to take a moment, place your finger on it, take a breath and imagine $100 going into your bank account. Get into the frequency and vibration of $100. You can start by thinking of what an extra $100 might give you. Perhaps you'll spend it on a new blouse, or invest in a new pair of shoes. Perhaps you'll give it to charity; whatever you plan on doing with it, feel into the feelings of what it's like to have it. To make it even more impactful, use all of your five senses for maximum effect.

chapter two:

YOU DON'T KNOW WHAT YOU DON'T KNOW

If you want to find the secrets of the Universe, think in terms of energy, frequency and vibration.

- Nikola Tesla

My dog Fergie likes to bark every time she hears something move outside the house. When Amazon comes to deliver a package, she goes off on a barking frenzy. It then causes a ripple effect in the building, in which the rest of the neighborhood dogs starts barking in unison. It's as if they're reminding each other how much they've got each other's back. Our neighbor Gale would walk by with her dog, Bentley (Fergie's arch nemesis) and in a quarter of a millisecond she acts like the world is coming to an end, yapping her scraggly tail off. I don't know if it's the Chihuahua in her, but whatever it is, Chihuahua or not, I decided that something needed to be done.

While surfing the web one week, I came across an advertisement that showed a remote control for dogs. Essentially what you do is point the black remote at the dog while it's barking and it will stop barking. A bit skeptical, I started going down the line of positive reviews of people claiming how much the remote changed the game for them, and they now can't imagine their lives without it. So, I caved and purchased the remote. Who would have thought that we went from remote control for inanimate objects like our TV, to remote controls for our pets?

A few weeks later, the dog remote came in the mail and I'm over the moon excited to use it! Luckily, someone walks by our balcony and Fergie went on her wild rant. I took the opportunity to take a step towards her, pointing the remote right at her and almost immediately she stopped barking. I was stunned.

This happened again later on that evening. The Amazon delivery guy drops off a package at the door and the moment he starts to walk away, Fergie starts yapping again, so I repeated the same steps as I did earlier that afternoon. Fergie instantly stopped barking, gives me a look, and walks quietly back to her dog bed.

By this time, I'm beyond fascinated, so I decided to do some more research on the dog remote. Believe me when I say, I have tried numerous ways to shush my dog down when she's barking only to be embarrassed (especially if we are in public) of how rare she actually listens to me. This was the first time that she actually stopped barking in a snap of a finger and it was something I couldn't wrap my head around, or didn't logically understand.

Upon further investigation, because I'm that type of person who wants to know the intricate details of why something happens the way it does, I discovered that the remote control emits a sound frequency that gets dogs attention. It's a sound frequency that humans can't hear!

Fun fact: Humans cannot hear sounds that vibrate at greater than 20,000 vibrations per second (20,000Hz). Meanwhile, dogs can hear sounds of up to 50,000 vibrations per second (50,000Hz). The remote I purchased was pretty much like a dog whistle emitting a sound greater than 20,000 Hz. That explains why dogs respond to a dog whistle while it appears completely silent to us.

The crazy thing is that I literally can't hear a single noise when I press the button. It's complete silence. To be honest, when I first received it, I thought the thing was broken. I kept pressing on the button, waiting for something miraculous to come out of it, but when I do press the button, I can see Fergie's ears go back as if she knew she did something wrong and she immediately goes to her dog bed and remains calm.

I mean, not just speaking as a dog mom, but this to me is complete proof that just because we can't physically hear, see, or touch something, it doesn't mean it doesn't exist. In fact, if you're significant other is a skeptic, think about love for instance. How do you even explain that gushiness? So, let's make it clear. Things may not "exist" in our reality, but it definitely exists, just not in our immediate paradigm per say.

Up until the 1900's our world has been operating from Newtonian physics. That means that we made calculations based off of our five physical senses. You got to see it to believe it was probably the motto that was thrown around by

Isaac Newton when he witnessed the apple fall from the tree and coined it the Law of Gravity. Whatever you see with your eyes is real and it's set. Since then, our world has operated in that way placing our logical minds at the forefront of our decision making.

Imagine being a cow herder on the Tibetan Plateau 60 years ago. Somebody shows up with blue light blockers and introduces you to solar panels. Or plays music on their iPhone. Or shows you a self-driving car. You'll think their nuts or its magic, right?

It wasn't until the discovery of quantum physics that scientists have begun to discover such things like the atom, subatomic particles, energy, and vibration. These are things that can't be seen with the naked eye but nonetheless exist. This is what we will be discussing in this chapter and how by knowing how the Universe works, we can then learn how to design the life we desire instead of falling victim to our circumstances.

I don't know where you stand when it comes to quantum physics – perhaps you have no idea what it even is, but if you've been trying to make more money doing all the things such as hustling, grinding and even taking on more work only to find yourself exhausted and still not a millionaire (yet), then it's time to really take a step back (even if it's just for this chapter) and rethink whether your current strategy is working for you.

A lot of people think that anything that can't be seen by the naked eye such as the new age term, Law of Attraction and energy work is a bunch of woo-woo fluff. I can admit that I was a bit of a skeptic to begin with. The thought of just sitting on your couch visualizing money floating effortlessly to you seems a bit too fairy tale-y. However, the more I started learning about it and now practicing it on a daily basis, I realized that quantum physics and the Law of Attraction isn't just about sitting and visualizing. It's actually like the dog remote I used on Fergie. Or the cow herder in the Tibetan Plateau. At first glance, it seems too good to be true. It's hard to believe, but once understood, it's like, why isn't this stuff taught in schools?

Just like I later realized that the real reason why my dog stopped barking wasn't because of some magical remote that I bought offline, but it was actually backed by science, it's time you understand the science behind all of this woo-woo stuff I'll be sharing with you for the rest of this book.

And really, the truth is, if you were to ask me, just like you can't build your dream house if you don't know what a house is made up of, you can't possibly build your dream life, one filled with abundance and financial freedom, without knowing what the Universe is really made up of. It's time to finally understand how everything works on a scientific and spiritual level. That is why I encourage you to continue reading this chapter with an open mind.

QUANTUM PHYSICS 101:

Have you ever wondered, what is the world made up of? What are we specifically made up of?

Let's start with you and me. Let's say you were to take a visit to a laboratory and pull up a microscope. You'll see that your body is made up of cells, and these cells are made up of molecules which are made up of atoms. Finally, on a deeper level, these atoms are made up of subatomic particles.

Obviously, you aren't able to see these subatomic particles but just know that at the very core and foundation, we are all made up of "large groups" of subatomic particles. Shocker. What you see is not what you get!

It's kind of like watching a movie premiere at the theaters. When you are watching the movie, you are seeing things move fluidly on the screen. You see the finished product. But what If I were to tell you that what you are seeing is only a cumulation of frames that contribute to the overall movie? For instance, there are 24 frames in one second of a movie. For you to see one second of a movie, it took 24 frames to make. That means in an hour film, 86,400 frames were taken and processed in your mind. But you can't see it because it's moving so fast. What this means is that the 86,400 frames you can't see are still considered a finished result. The only reason why you can't see it is because of the speed it is moving at. So, just like you can't see the frames in a movie, you can't see the subatomic particles that are vibrating within you and all around you. Remember, just because we don't see something doesn't mean it's not there.

Since these subatomic particles are moving at such a fast rate, you can begin to think of it all as large concentrations of energy. Everything is made out of subatomic particles which means that includes EVERYTHING, right? It's not just you. Your significant other, your friends, your pet, even the desk that you are using, the car that you are driving; they are all made up of large concentrations of subatomic particles aka energy packets or quanta.

Even your thoughts are made up of subatomic particles!

So, you may be thinking to yourself, if we are all made up of large concentrations of subatomic particles and we are essentially just energy, why does a chair look the way it looks and behave differently than let's say a human being? Well, the reason being, is that we are all vibrating at a different frequency, and that includes a piece of furniture, for example.

SO HOW DOES THIS ALL WORK?

Ok, let's explore how this all works and how we can actually start to design the life of our dreams with our newfound knowledge of quantum physics. So, when we think of subatomic particles, it's not in the common way we think of particles as an object. Your previous understanding of a particle may look like a grain of rice, or even a grain of sand. But you can't even see subatomic particles; they are not objects. Subatomic particles are basically "probabilities of existence" and can even be seen as "multiple existences" powered by intelligence and decision making.

There was a thought experiment done by a physicist named Schrodinger in which he placed a cat inside a box. He then placed a bomb inside the box that had a 50% chance of working. He then went ahead and placed a lid over the box. Is the cat dead or alive? There is no way of knowing whether or not the cat is alive or dead until we take off the lid to observe. While the cat is inside the box, the cat in quantum physics is said to be in a state of "multiple existences" or superposition. It is alive and dead at the same time. So, can you see how subatomic particles basically have "probabilities of existence" and is only powered by intelligence and decision making? It is only through making a decision to open the box to observe what is inside can we confirm the reality of the cat. Otherwise, it's in a state of potentiality.

Think of a TV show that you're absolutely obsessed with. Let's say you watch the Bachelor and the episode ends and there is a preview of what might unravel next week. You're sitting at the edge of your couch now just in a state of anticipation. There are so many possibilities that could happen. The Bachelor might choose the woman you are rooting for to stay on the show, or he'll send that same woman you had in mind to go home. You just don't know. In this case, these women on the show are "probabilities of existence." If they leave the show they don't exist for example, if they do stay, they exist.

Research into quantum mechanics has shown that the act of observing reality creates it. That only means one thing: Your belief and thinking is what creates matter. Attempting to observe something causes it to appear out of the nothing. Let's say you never got the chance to observe whether the cat in the box is alive or dead – the reality is only up to your interpretation. Simultaneously, the interesting thing is that if you are not aware of something, then it does not exist in your subjective reality.

For instance, in 2016 while I was backpacking across Europe, I met a girl who looked just like me. I immediately assumed she was Chinese but to be safe, I asked her where she was from. She then proceeded to tell me that she was from Kyrgyzstan. "But you look Asian!" I exclaimed. Turns out, Kyrgyzstan is a country in central Asia and I had no idea. If I hadn't met her, I would have lived the rest of my life not knowing there was a country called Kyrgyzstan. Prior to meeting her, I was oblivious to their culture, and people. The point is, your reality is based off of your thoughts and awareness of your reality. My reality may look completely different than yours and it wasn't until I observed something through my thoughts that is now part of my awareness.

The reason why things exist in reality for us is literally through our individual and collective thoughts.

Therefore, if no one paid attention to or gave any thought to the sun, for example, the sun would not exist in our reality.

So, if Quantum Physics clearly states that everything is made up of subatomic particles and that we essentially create our reality through observation, that only means that if we want to become the president for instance, it's possible. The only thing that is stopping you is your subconscious beliefs that are preventing you. Science has literally shown through Quantum Physics that we have direct control of our entire physical world. Remember, everything is through observation. If you are reading this right now and I'm telling you that it's completely 100% possible for you to become a millionaire but you silently scoff and think to yourself it's impossible, then can you see how you merely just created an observation without realizing it? If you scoffed at my statement, it's you further confirming that it won't happen for you.

You are the cause of your circumstances, including your experiencing of wealth or lack of it. Our thoughts are linked to this invisible energy and they determine what the energy forms. The more energetic charge and intention you put towards a thought, it becomes your reality. In fact, your thoughts literally shift the universe on a particle-by-particle basis to create your physical life and we can change the results of our lives and the environment through our observation and views of it.

Think about the last time you got into an argument with someone. That someone could be a friend, a significant other, or your mom. You observed that person's actions to be in a specific way based off of the story you gave it. Needing to vent and tell someone about the argument, you then turn to a friend and tell them what happened based off of your interpretation of it. Your friend confirms it to be true and the more you tell the story, it solidifies in your mind that you were right and your version of the story is truth, when in actuality everything was created in your mind.

Can you begin to now see that everything is created by you and you only? You are the cause of things instead of the effect. The reality is how you perceive it to be, so if you want it to exist – start perceiving it. And the possibilities are limitless!

Having all this in mind, we can now better understand how manifestation works: it's our unique and personal perception of reality that creates our reality and we draw into ourselves that which we perceive as real, because that's the most powerful way to influence our thoughts – by making our mind believe it's real.

LAW OF VIBRATION

With an open mind we can start to believe that something can be a reality even though we can't verify it with our five senses. Science has shown that everything is energy. You, me and everything else has its own vibrational frequency. This is called The Law of Vibration.

The Law of Vibration works just like how the Law of Gravity works which is each and every time without fail. Let's say you were to drop a watermelon off the 22nd floor of a building. As much as you want it to suspend in thin air, it's going to fall.

The Law of Vibration works the same way. The Law of Vibration states that everything in the Universe moves and vibrates – everything is vibrating at one speed or another. Nothing rests. Everything you see around you is vibrating at one frequency or another, and so are you. However, your frequency is different from other things in the universe and that´s why it seems like you are separated from what you see around you; people, animals, plants, trees and so on.

In truth you are not separated - you are in fact living in an ocean of energy - as we all are. We are all connected at the lowest level - The Unified Field. Everything has its own vibrational frequency: the table, the car, the picture frame, the rock - even our thoughts and feelings. It is all governed by The Law of Vibration.

You and everything else are just energy arranged together by information from the mind. Therefore, whatever opportunity it is that you want or whatever goal it is that you want to achieve, it's only a matter of aligning yourself to the frequency of what that goal or thing is vibrating at.

We are co-creators with the Universe. And if we are co-creators with Source energy, that only means one thing: We are not victims of our circumstances but rather, the captain of our lives.

In summary:

- Just because you can't see, hear, or touch something, it doesn't mean it does not exist.
- By understanding how the Universe works, you can begin to design and create the life that you desire.
- Science has shown through Quantum Physics that you are in direct control of your entire physical world.
- Your belief and thinking are what creates matter.
- You are the cause of your circumstances including your experiencing of wealth or lack of it.
- By raising your vibe and frequency, you can align yourself with situations and opportunities that are on that same frequency that you desire.
- If you are not aware of something, it does not exist in your subjective reality.

Your money mission:

To see how quantum jumping works first hand, try out the Two Glass Method. All you need to do is take two glass cups, drinking water, post its, and a marker. To begin, fill one glass with drinking water. Then, on a post-it note, in marker, right down your current situation. For example: I'd say something like I'm writing my first book. Then in another post-it note I'd write down my desired result I'd like to manifest. For me, it would be to be a #1 Amazon bestseller. Next, hold the cup with the current situation post it on it and that has water and think about the feelings of how you feel right now at this very moment. Really feel into those feelings while holding the cup. After a few minutes pour the water in the 'current situation' glass into the 'desired results' cup. Once you do that, repeat the process of holding the cup and emotionally charging the new cup with how you'll feel once your desired result has been achieved. Then, go ahead and drink the water.

To learn more about the two-cup method and quantum jumping watch a step-by-step tutorial here:

https://kristennoelle.co/bookresources

chapter three:

OLD, BROKE, AND SINGLE

Money and success don't change people;
they merely amplify what is already there.

-Will Smith

I was coaching one of my private clients one day, when the topic of raising her prices came up. I could immediately see the discomfort in her face as she nearly begged for us to talk about something else, which is an indication to me as a coach-that-kicks my-client's-behinds, that this very topic is definitely something we need to dive deep into.

A few days ago, she told me privately that her main focus at the moment was lowering her business expenses. I then asked her if the business expenses that she's planning on lowering is necessary to run her business and serve her clients at the quality she'd like it to be at.

There was a pause as she thought about my question and admitted to me a few moments later, that in order to maintain the quality of service she was giving her clients, she needed to keep those expenses.

"Okay, so what do you think you have to do then?" I asked.

"Well, I'll have to increase the revenue coming into my business." And then almost immediately she backed it up with: "BUT! That would mean I have to raise my prices."

I believe wholeheartedly that it is your moral obligation to make more money and become financially abundant, whether you are a business owner like my client, a freelancer, or someone who has a 9 to 5 job. In this chapter, I'm going to show you all the reasons WHY making money should matter to you, in ways you probably haven't even considered and why making more of it will not only help you personally, your family, and community, but also the entire world.

Your Health Depends Upon Your Financial Abundance

It is well known and documented that stress is the core root reason for all dis-ease. The more we stress out about things, the more cortisol we create which is a stress hormone. This is also known as the fight/flight response, where our bodies react to outside stimuli in order to prepare ourselves to either run, or fight.

And although that type of response was a very good

one to have for early man, in our modern world, it can wreak havoc on our immune system, and on our health.

When we're in a board meeting and suddenly we realize that things aren't going well, the body will respond as if it is being chased by a saber-toothed tiger. If we don't use up that extra energy boost of adrenalin and cortisol in our system, it can harm us rather than help us.

Most people equate money with stress because there never seems to be enough money. From this perspective, having plenty of money can definitely help to reduce the amount of stress that we have in our lives.

Having plenty of money allows you to have options that many others don't have. The amount of money that you have can have a direct impact on every aspect of your life, especially regarding your health.

When you have plenty of money, you'll be able to eat healthier, eat more organic type foods, and get the better-quality produce. You'll also be able to afford the more expensive, higher quality food restaurants.

Organic food is much more expensive than regular processed food, but if you don't have plenty of money, you'll be tempted to get the cheaper, less quality food that isn't nearly as good for you.

Not only will you be able to afford to eat healthier, but also, you'll be able to afford better healthcare. Healthcare can be incredibly expensive – especially when something very serious has been diagnosed and you need the best health care that money can buy.

When you have plenty of money, you can afford the better healthcare. And what is more important than your health?

But also, having plenty of money will allow you to be proactive with your health from the perspective of buying equipment or anything that could help you to stay in shape and stay in good health. When you have plenty of money, you can afford the best gym memberships, the best workout equipment, and the best of anything related to your health.

In addition to your physical health, when you have plenty of money, you can easily afford anything related to your mental and spiritual health. This means that you would be able to hire a life coach, or a therapist without worry about how much it cost, or anything related to keeping your mental state in tip-top condition...

But besides your physical and mental health, having plenty of money can also truly help you in your relationships too.

Let's cover that next.

The #1 Reason for Failed Relationships

Money can have a significant impact on our most important relationships – whether that be with a spouse, a significant other, and/or our family.

When money is tight, tension rises in any relationship. The additional problem is that many different types of negative feelings can come to the surface, such as feelings of inadequacy, blame, guilt, fear and even anger.

This is why money problems are the number one reason why marriages fail. Money problems are the number one reason why couples fight. And for most of us, we had parents who had fights about money.

It's not only the main reason for failed marriages – it's also the number one reason for failed relationships, and for the breakup of families. Most families have arguments because of a lack of money.

Can you think of any one thing that can have such a dramatic impact on relationships than money? It can either make a relationship a wonderful experience if there is plenty of money, or it can destroy any type of relationship, if there isn't.

The other kind of a relationship that money can have an impact on is your relationship with yourself. It takes money to cause the type of change that you want to have in your life.

So, a lack of money is the number one reason that relationships, marriages and families dissolve. Money can and will have a significant impact on any relationship. But what else can it affect?

What Will Be Your Legacy?

The money legacy that you build for yourself and your family now can have a major impact, not just on your children, but on your offspring for generations to come. You can literally change your children's future, including the future of your grandchildren, and great grandchildren – literally for generations to come. This is why it is so important to make the decision to create a legacy of thriving, instead of struggle.

If you look at the legacy of Theodor Seuss "Ted" Geisel who wrote the Dr. Seuss series of books, his legacy was writing successful books for children that became so popular, that they are still doing extremely well to this day.

The point is that you are either passing down a legacy of struggle for your children and generations to come, or a legacy of thriving. This is why money really does matter...

The other reason why it's so important for you to thrive with money instead of struggle is because if you're a parent, your children will pick up on your subconscious cues. Up until children are about seven years old, they are like sponges, soaking up everything as fact. But not only that, they also pick up on how you feel about money, and will develop the same beliefs about money that you do, for the most part.

This is another reason why it's very important for you to have a positive, healthy view of money. If your parents struggled with money, you can be the one who will break the chain of pain in your own family tree, so that your kids will have a positive and healthy view of money, now, and in the future.

Purpose and Contribution

We all were put here on planet earth in order to make a difference – we all have a unique purpose. And if we all lived up to our moral obligation of being financially abundant, as a result, there would be more than enough money to go around – and more solutions to the problems that we all face.

Most of us are not living up to this obligation. Most of us struggle when in reality, abundance was your birthright. You are a powerful creator and you're supposed to easily be able to create an abundant life. You are supposed to live a life of freedom, joy and excitement. You were never meant to struggle.

In addition, if you care about any type of a cause, you need to have real money. Money allows you to do so much for others, including donating to any charity that you believe in, or investing in any type of a cause that you want to help. It all takes money – real money...

And with money, you can build real change in your community. You could get involved in so many valuable projects and activities, right in your own community. The result would also be a real, true satisfaction that you support your local community, and feel that you are truly an important part of it.

If Money is Power...

If money is power, then who should have the power? The good guys like you, or the bad?

More of us good guys need to become rich, in order to counteract the not so good ones! There is nothing wrong with wanting or desiring to have more money – even outlandish amounts of money – especially if your intention is to do something good with it.

Too many bad guys have plenty of money and not enough good guys have it. It's time for change!

When you have the money, then you can use it for good.

That's the bottom line...

Your Happiness Depends on Money

They say that money can't buy happiness, but anyone who hasn't had any, and then does, might disagree. It's true that money itself isn't going to fulfill you as a person, but it sure can make life a lot more enjoyable and interesting. Not only that, but also, it's going to remove the stress that comes with not having enough money.

No longer will you stress out about being able to pay rent, buy food, buy the clothes that you really want, the home you really want, the car you really want. No longer will you have to worry about not being able to afford the proper gifts for family members during the holidays. There will be so many circumstances where you will realize that having money really does make life so much more stress-free and enjoyable.

So really, I'd say that our happiness does depend on money. Money affects every aspect of our lives. And when you don't have enough, you stress out about it all the time. To say that money can't buy you happiness is a bit misleading to say the least.

1,700 New Millionaires Every Day

There are 1,700 new millionaires made every single day (Bloomberg). That's a staggering amount. There has never been a better time in human history than right now to create an unlimited amount of abundance for yourself and your family.

The only reason why you may not be aware of this is because it may not be in your paradigm right now. But when you shift your paradigm to believing that it is possible to become a millionaire, then it can become true – you can create that reality.

The results that you have in your life right now are a result of the decisions, beliefs and thoughts you have been using. So, if you don't like your results, then first change your thoughts and beliefs about what is possible for you.

Belief is everything. You get what you believe you can get. You get what you expect to get. And when you believe it, you'll see it as Dr. Dyer used to say.

In summary:

- Your health depends on your financial abundance. The more abundant you are financially, the more you can afford to take care of yourself.

- Stress is the number one cause of disease and financial stress is the number one reason couples fight. By learning how to be financially abundant, you can minimize any arguments related to lack of money.

- Your children's future depends on your relationship with money. Will you pass on a legacy of thriving or struggling for money?

- It's possible for you to become financially abundant. In fact, there are 1,700 new millionaires that are born a day. Why can't you be one of them?

Your money mission:

Take out a sheet of notebook paper or simply pull up a favorite journal of yours and begin to write down all the reasons WHY it's important for you to make more money. What will having more money mean for you, your family and your community? How will your family benefit from you making even more money? What will your contribution look like?

chapter four:

THE PRICE OF YOUR DREAMS

Intention is one with cause and effect. Intention determines outcome. And if you're stuck and not moving forward, you have to check the thought and the action that created the circumstance.

- Oprah Winfrey

There's an app that you can download onto your phone called Bumble BFF that will basically match you up with a new friend. All you have to do is build out your profile and just like any other dating app, your thumb makes all your conscious decisions for you. It's kind of like Tinder but instead of looking for a potential lover, you're basically looking for a friendship.

Despite what everyone was telling me, on how lame the idea was, I of course ignored all the naysayers and went ahead and created a profile with the intention of finding like-minded girlfriends. Turns out, what I intended was exactly what I was looking for: amazingly, brilliantly curated, handpicked friends, who thought the same as me, liked the same things as me, and had the same ambitions and goals – all through this one app.

I must have spent a few hours prior to downloading the app in which I pulled out a piece of paper and got super, crystal, clear on what type of friend I wanted to bring into my life. And because I took that extra step, I now have friends that I met through the app that matched up to my expectations as to what I wanted from a friend.

What most people don't realize is that you can do the same exact thing with money. Remember that all money is, is energy. When energy is directed with a clear purpose, that's when you can see the results much quicker. You'll come to realize that when you give money a purpose, the more it will come to you and that you'll attract. And as cliché as this may sound, every penny has a purpose.

Just like dating without a clear intention will result in you attracting a man or woman that is not exactly what you are looking for, same goes for wanting money but not knowing what you'll do with it once you have it.

Keep Money Moving 

Believe it or not, the whole purpose of money is to keep it moving. Don't believe me? Let's look at the word currency in the Merriam Webster dictionary.

Currency. 1a: circulation as a medium of exchange.

Just like a water current is supposed to move in a definite direction, same goes with money. It's smart and advisable to save money for a rainy day, but just like water, your house is only big enough to save X amount of water. Ideally, you want to know that you have enough money in which the more you put out, the more it comes back to you.

However, if you don't control the flow of water, it can get quite messy. Just like water, when you have no idea the direction of where money is going, you'll end up with a mess in your bank account.

So, while it's attractive to make even more money, if you don't know where that extra money will go towards, then why do you think it will be given to you?

It's kind of like if I were to give you a gift, and that gift was a new wallet. Imagine you accepted the gift but you didn't even use it. It was left sitting there in your bottom drawer. Honestly, I wouldn't want to give you any more gifts.

The Universe works the same way. Each day, we are given a gift. When we don't appreciate the gift that was given to us, the Universe will not give us more. On top of all that, if you aren't intentional with what you'll do with the gift aka money, why would the Universe want to give you more of it?

How to Give Your Money a Purpose

1) Get clear on how much you want to bring in.

The truth is, if you aren't clear on what it is that you want, more than likely, whatever it is that you want is not going to come into your life. That applies to everything in your life, including money. But the more specific you can get on the exact number it is that you want to make each month, then that's when you can basically expedite the process.

2) Get clear on the reasons WHY you want the money.

Remember that everything needs to have a clear purpose and intention. If you're not clear why you are doing something then it doesn't make sense for you to do it. Assigning reasons for why you want more money, for example, doesn't have to be something life changing like donating money to charity. In fact, there's no right or wrong way to do this.

Say you want to get your nails done each week and you want money to do that, and by doing your nails each week, you just feel good about yourself – that's enough reason for wanting it. The point is though, it's absolutely crucial for you to know your reasons for wanting the money and that it makes you feel good.

3) Ask yourself -- where is it going?

Without knowing where your money is going each month, it's kind of like asking for more candy during Halloween when you were a child. The Universe can see candy stockpiled beside you as you try to figure out what to do with it. Should

I stuff it all inside my mouth, or store it in my bedroom? You're overwhelmed enough with the pile and giving you more candy would only mean signing yourself up for candy suicide.

As a parent, you wouldn't do that to your child. Neither would the Universe. That's why it's absolutely crucial for you to know where exactly the money you are making is going to. Is it going to the debt you still owe? 10% of it to charity? Perhaps it's to the course you've been wanting to invest in. Giving clear containers for your money to flow into will send a signal to the Universe that you are ready for more and you know how to direct the flow of money traffic.

4) Get specific on the details. 

Wanting an extra $5000 in your bank account each month so you can move to a larger condo is great and all, but how can you get EVEN more specific as to what it is that you want out of a condo? Most people would go shopping for a condo after the $5000 is consistently coming through their bank account, but what I highly suggest is doing the shopping beforehand. When you get super crystal clear on the specifics of what it is that you want and why you want it, this again expedites the process. Again, details truly matter, and when you can get down to the specifics, so much so that you can literally close your eyes and imagine the details of what you'll be using the money for, down to the color of your shirt you'll be wearing when you treat your parents out for sushi, that's when you'll start seeing the results you've been looking for.

In summary:

- When energy is directed with a clear purpose, that's when you can see the results much quicker.

- When we don't appreciate the gift that was given to us, the Universe will not give us more.

- You have to get clear on why, where, and how much.

Your money mission:

To make this simple, get crystal clear on the amount you'd like to attract in the next three months. Follow the steps suggested for you above. Remember to be as specific as possible. The more specific and detailed you are, the faster results you'll achieve.

chapter five:

ABUNDANCE: EXPLAINED

As long as we remain vigilant at building our internal abundance—an abundance of integrity, an abundance of forgiveness, an abundance of service, an abundance of love—then external lack is bound to be temporary.

- Marianne Williamson

I remember being a teen and going to the liquor store with my dad for the first time.

My parents both don't drink any alcohol so going to a liquor store was a rare occurrence. However, my parents were throwing a party that evening, and my Uncle Michael wanted a specific type of alcohol that Costco didn't carry, and that's how we ended up at the liquor store.

We were at check out and I remember seeing lottery tickets for the first time. I asked my dad what they were and after he explained the basic concept, he basically told me that lottery tickets were bad news. It didn't make sense to me at the time, because in my mind, I'm thinking, what's so bad about winning money? However, in my dad's eyes, he explained to me that according to the news 70% of lottery winners go broke after two years of winning the lottery and sometimes even worse.

My dad's concern and fear were that he would end up like the people who lost all their winnings, get robbed and possibly lose everything he owned in the process.

But what people don't realize is that it's not the money that makes you rich or wealthy.

It's your financial thermostat.

Your Financial Thermostat

Your financial thermostat is not much different than the thermostat you have in your house that controls the temperature. If you set your thermostat in your house to 70 degrees and the temperature falls below that, the heat will kick on. And if it goes above that, the heat will turn off and maybe even the air will turn on. Your systems are always working to keep your house at the temperature you set on the thermostat.

Here's an example of what I mean:

Let's say that you are used to seeing $5000 in your

bank account. You suddenly get a promotion. Unless you change your financial thermostat, you will either spend or lose that extra money so that you are back to seeing the $5000 in your bank account.

Don't believe me? Look at your bank account balance now. What number is it always hovering around no matter what you do every month? That number that you see, is where your financial thermostat is set at.

Your financial thermostat is so ingrained that, whether you experience a major setback or amass a large fortune, ultimately you will find yourself at the number that you feel most comfortable with. That also explains why lottery winners are so often broke again in two years. If your financial thermostat is set for "Broke," any wealth that comes to you will be a memory before you know it.

On the other hand, if your financial thermostat is set for "Abundance," you will move through any financial reversals and regain (or exceed) your high level of prosperity with ease and grace. Think about Donald Trump for instance. Even though at one point he was more than $2 Billion in debt, his financial thermostat is set for "Billionaire!" and he was able to make that amount back again to his estimated net worth of $5 Billion.

That's why if you want to acquire any type of wealth and attract more money, first and foremost, you must work with your wealth consciousness. I will explain that further in this chapter, but the first step is to become aware of your financial thermostat.

Once you are aware of your financial thermostat, then it's a matter of making a choice to make changes to your wealth consciousness by firstly adopting more of a growth mindset rather than a reduction mindset.

You see, what most people are programmed to do is to cut back when times get tough. We've been taught as a society that instead of thinking of possibilities, to limit ourselves, especially when it came down to money. I, for one, was surrounded with that type of mentality. As a child I would see my parents cut back on expenses whenever an unexpected emergency would hit our household.

Let's say for example you were hit with an unexpected doctor's bill. Naturally, most people will see it as a setback and find ways to cut back their lifestyle in order to pay for the bill, kind of like what I was taught to do as a child. Although it doesn't seem like a big deal, I want you to think about how much you can cut back before you can't cut back any further.

When you train your brain to automatically revert to cutting back, you are operating from a state of lack. And since money is not attracted to lack energy, cutting back will send a signal to the Universe that you want more lack.

Rather, being in a growth mindset means shifting the way you see a situation and asking yourself how you can make more money in a situation like this, when you are hit with an unexpected medical bill per say.

How to Alter Your Thermostat

The first step to altering your financial thermostat is to think in terms of expansion rather than contraction. The moment we start limiting ourselves and what's possible for us, we go into this never-ending cycle of lack. After all, if you really think about it, how much can you possibly cut down when you are already cutting down? Whereas when we train our mind to be expansive, the opportunities can be endless. It's only until we break out of this cycle that we are able to start building our wealth consciousness.

Thinking that there isn't enough, is going to prevent you from accumulating wealth because it will continue to put you in that vibration of lack.

So how can you get yourself out of that lack mentality and into more of a growth mindset?

Well you can start by asking yourself how you can provide more value to the world.

If the world seems too much of a stretch for you at the moment, you can start off small. Look in terms of your community, your current job, or even solving a current problem that you know other people are struggling with that's dear to your heart.

Essentially there is a law that states that the more impact and value we give others, the more it comes back to us.

Think about the world's richest people. They provide value to millions of people from the consumer purchasing the product down to the employee working for the company. Therefore, the more people you impact, the more wealth is accumulated. You can start by asking yourself, what value can I provide to others? How can I make a difference in my community?

In summary: 

- It's not money that makes you wealthy or not – it's your wealth consciousness.
- To change your financial situation, start by changing your financial thermostat.
- Train yourself to have a more growth mindset rather than a reduction mindset.
- The more value you give others, the more it comes back to you.

Your money mission:

Start by going into your bank account today and see what number is present. Ask yourself honestly if your bank account is always hovering around this specific number. From there, think about how you can increase that number by giving more value either in your place of work or in your business. To take this to the next level, think about your own unique qualities and how that can be of value to someone else. Make a list of 20 or more unique qualities of yours that can be of value to others.

chapter six:

THE REAL, REAL, TRUTH ABOUT MONEY

We can't solve problems by using the same kind of thinking we used when we created them.

- Albert Einstein

I think it's safe to say that nobody wants to grow up being a "bad person." So, when I realized for the first time ever, when I was seven years old during dinner one night, that sales people were "bad people," I swore to myself I never wanted to sell anything to anyone as long as I was alive on this earth.

We were all gathered for dinner one night; me, my little brother, my mom and dad and right when we were about to take a bite of the delicious salmon my mom baked for us, the phone rang. My dad, frustrated, got out of his seat and walked over to the home phone. I could see the annoyance in my dad's furrowed brows as he angrily hung up on the person that was on the other line.

When he got back to the dining table, my mom naturally asked who it was as my dad replied, "Damn salespeople, always trying to sell me." My brother and I looked across the table at each other, bit our lips and kept quiet, afraid to make our dad even angrier. That night, the four of us ate our dinner in complete silence.

That wasn't the only instance my dad would be in a crabby mood. My entire childhood I would see my dad frustrated whenever it was a telemarketer or sales person on the other line. It then became a common occurrence in which he would even stay silent when he picked up the phone and wait until the other person on the line said something first. The moment my dad found out it was a sales person, he would punch on the keypads of the phone so that there would be a loud pinging noise for the other person to hear on the other side.

Watching my dad do that numerous times as a child solidified the belief in me that salespeople and the act of selling came from the devil himself and if I were to ever do any type of selling, I would pretty much go to hell.

My Own Nagging Belief

Fast forward eighteen years later when I decided I wanted to go into life coaching and realized that part of becoming a life coach meant that I had to sell my own services. Boy, was I in for a rude awakening. Here I was, passionate about helping people transform their lives and yet deep down, I had this nagging belief that selling to others meant I was doing damage to their lives.

When you have a strong belief, it can prevent you from taking any type of action.

Basically, what I was going through and what you might be familiar with is something called split energy. Split energy is when your thoughts, beliefs, feelings (both conscious and subconscious) and actions are not 100% aligned with one another. Hence the "split" in the energy. It's hard to move forward 100% with something and get the results you desire when you have split energy. It's kind of like trying to be in two places at the same time. It's simply not possible. Well, technically it's possible if physically you are in one place and mentally you are someplace else, BUT think about how productive you can actually be if you aren't fully in one place: mind, body, and spirit.

You might have split energy with money or the idea of what money is, at this very moment. In fact, I think it's safe to assume you do, because if you didn't, you wouldn't be reading this book.

In fact, you may have the same belief as me that selling is a horrible act which is preventing you from truly selling your own products or services. Think about it. If you believed selling is bad for over twenty years, even though now you know consciously that selling is not all bad, your subconscious mind is nagging at you to stay true to your values – in other words, to be a good person and not sell.

Or, you may have the belief that money causes pain and stress because you grew up seeing your parents fight about money. So, why would you, in your right mind, invite chaos and arguments into your life, right?

Or maybe you'll find your childhood similar to mine, where there was never enough, where even showers were limited to five minutes at a time. So, you resort to hoarding and saving your money for a rainy day, blocking money from flowing in and out of your bank account.

If those experiences did happen to you when you were a child, subconsciously you may have held onto your truths about what money is and it's now affecting you from receiving, attracting and even earning and making money. It would make a lot of sense as to why even as much as you desire more money, it's not showing up for you.

Your Money Belief Roots

All the primary beliefs we have around money, come from what we feel, see and hear as children. In our earliest years, up until our conscious minds kick in at age six or seven with concepts of right and wrong, true and false, we accept what we experience as "truth." So, unless we have a reason to revisit a belief as we grow up and consciously change it, we carry many beliefs forward that came directly from our parents and other figures of authority in our early lives (teachers, neighbors, counselors, preachers – anyone of an authority figure, for example).

Remember that our first interaction with money was with our very first money teachers. In my case, they were my parents. They were the ones who taught me everything I needed to know about money. Just like I described in the story above, you may have picked up a story about money from your parents. And it's not always just our parents – it could also be the environment where you grew up or other adults you've interacted with as a child. Like I mentioned before, from the ages of 0-7, we are literally like sponges. We pick up EVERYTHING and ANYTHING.

Our Money Programming

So why is it that our programming from childhood is so long-lasting? Between the ages of birth to seven, we are essentially in a trance-like state, absorbing everything around us like sponges. Children are subconsciously picking up and storing everything that the adults around them are doing, feeling and saying in order to figure out how to navigate their own world. Our sense of identity and who we are to become in the future is very much contingent upon our early subconscious programming.

That also explains why if we are not aware and clean up our subconscious beliefs that pretty much operate 95% of our being, we end up just like our parents in some way, shape or form.

But sometimes it can go beyond what we remember as children. If you really want to understand the belief that your parents have about money, look into your ancestral baggage around money. We might also find some very old patterns driving our behaviors – so old they almost feel etched into our DNA.

Before you reach for your phone right now to call your parents and blame them for how much they ruined your life, it's important to understand that all your parents were doing was repeating what they learned to be true from their parents. Basically, your parents were doing the best they could with what they had at the time.

Do you now see why it's so important for YOU to break the chain of beliefs that might be leaving your family in a state of struggle instead of a state of thriving?

The great news is that even though it was not your fault that all of these beliefs were passed onto you as a child, you have a choice whether or not to believe them moving forward. More importantly, it's up to you to actually reprogram yourself so that you believe new beliefs and thoughts that are serving you.

The Real Truth About Money 

The truth about money is that it will always be subjective to you. Whether you think money is hard to come by or easy to make is entirely 100% true. Whatever you believe about money will become true in your life. What may be true to you may not be true for me. But none of that matters. What matters now is what you choose to do moving forward.

I once had a client who wholeheartedly believed that the only people that were making real money online were people who were teaching other people how to make money online. During one of our sessions together, she pulled out all the evidence she found that solidified this belief she had.

Now deep down, I knew this belief was not true, because I actually had friends that were making a lot of money online and they were not teaching people how to make money online. I challenged my client to question this belief of hers which she reluctantly did. It wasn't until we really looked into her beliefs and picked it apart that she realized that this belief she held was preventing her from taking any action in her business.

Therefore, what is the real truth about money? Is money the root of all evil? Does money grow on trees? Is money easy to make? Hard to make? Does money flow easily and effortlessly to you? The ultimate truth is up to you. Whether you believe it to be true or not, is entirely on your side of the court. You get what you believe is true.

In summary:

- From the ages of 0-7 we are like sponges, soaking up anything and everything around us, including the thoughts, beliefs and actions of others.
- Truths about money are relative and subjective to you.
- You are the only person 100% responsible for who you decide to become moving forward.
- Our parents did the best they could with the resources they had at the time – stop blaming them for why you are the way you are now.
- Our money beliefs are passed down to us from our money teachers and now it's up to us to change those beliefs we've held onto for so long.

Your money mission:

Take a moment and write down all the money beliefs you feel is absolutely true at this moment. A great way to do this is actually visit your parents if you can and start talking to them about the subject of money. See what comes up, what kind of feelings, stories or reactions are made, when the topic of money is discussed. Don't judge what comes up but rather, objectively look at things as if you are just taking notes with no judgment. Notice all the money beliefs that show up when you actually shine a light on them.

chapter seven:

MONEY LESSONS DISGUISED AS BLESSIN'S

A lesson is repeated until learned.

- Cherie Carter Scott

My friend Emily and I were playing Bubble Charms on our way back to LA from Nashville, Tennessee. If you've never played the game before, it's quite addicting – especially if you're super competitive like I am. Before I continue on with the story, I have to disclose that I am not one of those people that download games on their smartphone and play on a daily basis. In fact, the only time I play any type of video game, or even games in general, is on that rare occasion when someone challenges me to it. In this case, it was when my friend Emily gave me a competitive look an hour into our flight and when this happens, my competitive nature awakens and I can't help but say aloud, "Game on, sister."

Emily has clearly played the game many times over, as she explains to me how to play Bubble Charms. "So, all you do is create and burst groups of matching bubbles. Your goal is to reach the highest level and get a high score. When you remove bigger groups and earn 500 points, you get to go onto the next level."

I'm thinking to myself, okay that's easy enough, I'm just going to keep matching bubbles with their corresponding colors.

Five minutes into the game, and that's when I realize it's a bit more challenging than I thought it was going to be. Not only do I have to match colors like I'm in 3rd grade, but the bubbles are coming down at me like a ton of bricks and if I don't earn the 500 points, by the time they all fall down, I just continue to stay at this level and I don't advance. I look over at Emily and she's easily and strategically matching bubbles like it's a stroll at the park.

Before I know it, the bubbles come down at me and I lose. Emily advances to the next level as I discouragingly look at my screen as the button *"play again?"* pops up at me. I'm not one to quit so I play again. Round two baby.

Life is Like a Game

Believe it or not, life can be looked at as a game. For example, if you take away our emotions, our ego, our attachments to what so and so said about us during Aunt Sally's family reunion, life is definitely a game. The reason why some people are better at life's game is because they have learned to master the challenges that were thrown at them. They then proceed to advance to next levels which again they are presented with a set of new challenges/lessons.

The only real difference is that in real life, we are often clouded by our own emotions and the judgements of others. Emotions such as fear and self-doubt plague us as we think to ourselves whether or not we "are good enough" to even play. Our ego often gets in the way of this game we call "life," which explains why we subconsciously self-sabotage our efforts whenever we get close to success – at least that's what I realized through my own experience, and by coaching my clients.

Really, the sad part is NOT that people don't know the rules of the game; it's literally as if they are saying that they know the rules of the game, but they don't think they are smart enough, pretty enough, or rich enough to play and therefore they can't play.

Imagine playing a video game in which the character inside the game is always self-doubting their ability to beat the challenges thrown at them in the game. Even if you do have unique gifts and powers that could potentially beat the other player, the sheer thought of self-doubt has already prevented any chance of winning. Do you see how your life is literally just a game? Your emotions are fogging up your potential to win in life!

Lessons to be Learned

I've often questioned a lot when I was younger why I was given the parents I have. Why was my dad so frugal and cheap and why I couldn't be born into a rich family? It wasn't until I came across Cherie Carter-Scott's book, "If Life is a Game, These Are the Rules" that I realized that the challenges and hardships that were presented to me in my life were nothing but lessons that were designed specifically for me.

I want you to think of what's currently keeping you stuck from making the amount of money you desire. What exactly is your current money challenge? With every challenge there is a lesson that is presented to you. Most people will think of it as a nuisance or an unfortunate event, but what most people don't realize is that the challenge that is presented before you is the thing you need to overcome, in order for you to advance to the next level in life. Also, that disguised within that challenge is an opportunity for growth.

An easier way to describe this, so that you have a clear visual in your mind, is to think of income levels. Let's say for example, once you have made $50,000 you can advance to level two and the moment you make $100,000 you have made it to level three. Again, these are just examples for you to visualize.

The challenges and lessons that you will face leading up to making $50,000 will be different types of challenges and lessons you'll face on your way to making $100,000 – even more so if you were someone working at a 9-5 job compared to someone trying to be their own boss. The types of discipline and habits needed are different and if you are currently stuck at a certain level that you can't breakthrough, that's the money lesson that's presented to you. Now, it's really your job to learn from it so it won't be repeated.

Remember, there is no such thing as a mistake. It may seem like a mistake at the moment but really, everything is a lesson. The more you view your life situations as lessons, the faster you'll advance to the next level. Trust me when I say this, because I have had first-hand experience. I have repeated several lessons before simply because of my refusal to learn from them at the moment.

You may think, well why would anyone want to repeat lessons or challenges if they know that it's only going to be repeated again and again until they learn? Two reasons really: Number one, changing isn't particularly the most comfortable thing. In order for you to actually learn your lesson and advance to the next level, it will require an uncomfortable amount of growth and change. Most people are not willing to go through the discomfort temporarily to see the light at the other end. More importantly, our ego tricks us into thinking that it's better to stay safe and small because it's trying to protect us.

The second reason is that sometimes we must repeat the same lesson until we finally get it. That also explains why some people date the same type of man or woman that doesn't serve them, until they gain awareness and consciously break the cycle that they are in. Again, it's not about giving up on love. It's not like you've been hurt so many times that you have thrown your hands up in the air and declared that love isn't for you.

However, when lessons repeat themselves, it's only a sign that we haven't learned that particular lesson yet and it's showing itself up to you in order for you to partake in the opportunity for growth. It's kind of like life saying to you, "Hey! The next level of your life is waiting for you – you just need to learn this lesson!!"

How do we advance to the next level and actually learn our lesson?

1) Acknowledge that mistakes are just lessons.

Most of us get so wrapped up with our mistakes that we actually take it at face value and allow our mistakes to define us as human beings. We can start getting into the habit of seeing our mistakes as only lessons so that we can get through the pain much faster and not beat ourselves up over it like I did many times over.

Growing up, mistakes were not welcomed in my family. I was brought up to think that if you made a mistake, you were basically doomed for life and that the world was going to end. That created a lot of pressure for me to be perfect or in other words achieve perfectionism. Instead of seeing mistakes as lessons, I saw mistakes as something I needed to avoid and that it said something about me when I made them.

For example, when I came across my first unhappy client, I saw this "mistake" as a sign that I shouldn't be coaching people. In my eyes, every single one of my clients must be happy or that would mean I did something wrong; I made a mistake and what would that say about me? How could I possibly show up and help people if I was making people unhappy, right? After a month of beating myself up, I realized that this was the lesson that I needed to learn - that if I was to stay in business, there will be people that won't like me or be unhappy with my service. It wasn't until I fully learned this lesson that I was able to move forward.

2) Step back and see what money incident keeps repeating in your life right now.

Is it that you keep getting the same types of clients that flake on you and don't take your work seriously? Maybe you can't break a monthly income level that you've been trying to get past for half a year. Or perhaps the moment you get a little bit of success, something happens which makes you go back to where you started. Think of whatever you are going through right now that prevents you from getting to that next level in your life. I want you to actually get super crystal clear on what it is. It's only by gaining awareness that you can even start fixing the problem. Without awareness, all else suffers.

3) Change your beliefs to match up with the solution of your problems.

Einstein once said that we can't solve problems using the same level of thinking that we used when we created them. What does that tell you? That must mean that if you find yourself repeating the same lesson in your life over and over and over again right now, you are still stuck at a certain level of thinking that is preventing you from achieving, let alone, attracting the certain level of success that you want in your life right now. What most people do is that they start doing more; they start working harder, doing all of these things with the current mindset that has given them their current results.

I'm a firm believer that if you want to advance to the next level, it's time to admit that it's not about doing more and being busier. It's time to dig deep and transform those beliefs and your thoughts so that you can advance to that next level of your life. That's why in Pillar Two, Money Minded, we are going to completely rewire your thoughts and beliefs so that you are prepared for every level that you may face.

In summary:

- Life is like a game.
- There are lessons for you to learn specifically for you.
- The challenges that are presented before you are the same things you need to overcome.
- There is no such thing as a mistake – they are just lessons.
- Change will require an uncomfortable amount of growth.
- You must change your beliefs in order to match the solution.

Your money mission:

Take a moment and ask yourself honestly, what you feel is your current money lesson and what is being shown to you that you need to overcome during this time. Remember that whatever money challenge is presented to you at this time, is there for a very specific reason. Instead of ignoring the messages and nudges that are coming up in your life right now, go through it and look at it from an objective point of view.

Pillar Two:

YOUR MONEY MINDSET

chapter eight:

THE #1 SECRET FOR A FRESH START

To forgive is to set a prisoner free and discover that the prisoner was you.

- Lewis B. Smedes

I remember the very first online money workshop I hosted. I had about five people participate with me and it was more transformative than I thought it would ever be. What it made me realize was that even though the five people that were in this workshop with me swore that they wanted to create new, healthier, and happier relationships with money so that they could attract and bring more of it into their lives, they had a lot of blame towards either themselves or others that prevented them from moving forward.

It was literally as if heavy chains were pulling them backwards, into their past, anchoring them into their outdated money beliefs. They all had shameful secrets, unresolved family or relationship drama that involved money, down to the practical "to do's" they haven't yet checked off their list.

And as genuinely as they desired to create a new future, one filled with abundance, they simply could not move forward until they were able to look into their past, address what was tying them to it, and allow themselves to let go.

Your Money Skeletons

Here's what I have found that worked for myself and my clients each and every time: when we can look back at our pain from the past (whatever that might be), honor it, and release it, we can move forward in new and liberated ways.

In this chapter, we are going to work through forgiveness, completions and letting go. In order to build a better future, one of abundance, you must begin by cleaning up your past. I rolled my eyes the first time I learned that I had to do this work, but it wasn't until I surrendered and actually looked at my past and forgave it, that I was really able to move forward.

So, you might be thinking to yourself, how does forgiving myself and others actually help me attract and make more money?

We cannot move forward attracting and making more money when we have money skeletons stored away in our closet. Temporarily, it may be possible but eventually, stored negative emotions will always bubble up to the surface to be dealt with. Instead of waiting for that day to come, why not choose to take care of it now?

First of all, I understand how uncomfortable it can be to look at past memories that might trigger feelings that you weren't planning on revisiting. However, those stored away awful memories is what's preventing you from moving forward. Consciously on a daily basis, you may not be thinking of the things that are hurting you. But subconsciously, until you have learned to release and forgive the money stories that you have held onto all this time, it will continue to show up in your life.

We all have money incidents, situations or stories that we have to forgive. Sometimes, those incidents that affect us aren't directly related to money but somehow, they are tied to your capability to attract more abundance.

For instance, in my previous job, I was sexually harassed in a hotel room by my manager at the time. I carried that feeling of shame and embarrassment for a long time thinking that if I just ignored it, it would eventually go away. I call that putting sprinkles on top of dog poop. A lot of people would rather save the time of cleaning up the poop and go and buy some sprinkles that they could cover up, hoping things will be okay. Unfortunately, it doesn't work that way.

What I noticed was that after that sexual harassment incident, I mistrusted men in the workplace. I allowed that one incident to define how I viewed men and that prevented me from being able to even work effectively with the opposite sex.

Naturally when one is not able to work effectively, you can guess how this affected me financially.

How to Cut Your Money Cords

Many of us have anxious and negative attachments to people and situations who have hurt us. This is like a cord that attaches us to the perpetrator in a negative way and is based on anger, hate, resentment and sometimes mixed with irrational guilt or shame. This could create a love-hate type of a feeling and an internal conflict or even split energy.

All of these are heavy and negative toxins that need to be released. But when you cut this cord between you and the perpetrator, you feel liberated, you feel light, and you feel like a new person. This internal transformation makes you more open to the positive things that life has to offer. When you let the cord hold you back, it slows you down from moving forward. That is why you have to cut the cord through forgiveness.

Forgiving someone also doesn't mean you are saying what he/she did was right. Forgiveness is both having grace and also releasing yourself from the situation. It's recognizing that mistakes have been made and that it's important to move on, since it doesn't define us.

So, let me ask you, what are some of the money incidents or dramas that you have to forgive?

I'll give you some examples of the money stories that I personally had to forgive:

My Money Stories

For instance:

"My partner financially supported me for several months when I decided to quit my job after being sexual harassed and the guilt was killing me."

"My dad taught me to be mean to telemarketers growing up, and now I can't help but feel a certain way towards sales people."

"The time my family got into a car accident in Hong Kong, and my uncle who was driving the car asked us not to claim insurance."

"The time I was seven years old and stole a pen from Marshalls."

"The time I was late paying my assistant."

These are just a few of the many money stories I have carried with me, that I needed to forgive. We all have money situations, stories or people we need to forgive. It's time for you to rediscover some money stories that you would have to forgive in order for you to move forward.

You are not alone in having money stories or secrets – we all have them and it's time for us to let them go. We all have our "money stuff" from the past that needs to be grieved, completed, released, and forgiven.

So, after this chapter, I want you to start listing out all your money stories. Spend some time doing this. I want you to think about the money shame that feels raw, or blame that's possibly draining your energy such as: loose ends you desperately want to tie off, and money beliefs that you've outgrown.

By writing all of these stories down and listing them, it opens the door to completion in order to progress forward.

So, when we let go of old beliefs about money and choose what new beliefs, we bring forward with us, into the future, we not only release the old pain, we also uncover surprisingly wonderful gifts.

Here's a word of advice: forgiveness requires work. It is a journey. Forgiveness is non-linear, fluid, deeply personal, often mysterious, and undertaken by the brave few. But the rewards, my friend, are huge.

How and What to Forgive

Forgive yourself. Forgive your parents. Forgive that rude collections agent. Forgive the IRS. Forgive society. Forgive your ancestors for what they did and what they didn't do.

Remember that forgiveness is not FOR other people – it's for yourself to choose not to feel those emotions anymore.

Forgive yourself for being messy, for not knowing better, for knowing better, but doing it anyway.

Forgive yourself for not making more money. For making more money than you feel comfortable with. For racking up debt. For being a stay-at-home mom instead of an entrepreneur. For being an entrepreneur instead of a stay-at-home, mom. For not living up to your parents' expectations.

Forgive yourself for the big things and the little things. For the obvious, subtle, and secret things.

No act of forgiveness is too small if it liberates energy for you.

Let go of the anger and hurt and regret and stuck-ness. Look at it all, bless it, thank it, and let it go.

Grieve. Grieve that money that's gone. Grieve that the chapter of your life that ended too soon. Grieve that friendship you lost. Grieve those paths you never took. Let it out, but then let it go.

Complete your unfinished business. Tie up those loose ends draining your energy.

Release your shame. Release the pain. Release the guilt. Let it all go.

The 6-Step Process to Forgive

The following is my 6-step process to forgiveness and how by following this framework, you'll be able to release the energy that's been holding you back so that you can completely heal from your past.

1) Pull out a piece of paper and do a huge brain dump.

However, you choose to do this, remember to define who and what it is that you need to forgive. It could have been money situations involving other people, or even just yourself. Identify the person who has affected you negatively towards money and with whom you still have an anxious attachment, physically or emotionally. Then, identify the specific behavior that damaged you. Be precise and clear about this. Write everything down and reflect on it. There's really no right or wrong way to do this. Anything that you can remember that has contributed to your negative thoughts, feelings or beliefs around money, write it all down.

2) Let the feeling be felt and ask to see things differently.

Any feelings that are attached to the damaging behavior need to be brought to the surface. You need to find a safe place to do this, to let the feeling out and to process it, to release these toxins. If you need to cry, do so. If you need to get angry, find a safe place to let the anger out. Then it's all about shifting your perspective. Ask the Universe to show you how you can see the situation or person differently.

This is such a powerful question because it allows you to see things objectively and from another point of view. Sometimes when we are so stuck in our perspective, we can't see things objectively. Remember, there is no need to make the person the behavior, but remember that the behavior is a part of that person. Think of the person as a whole person with positive and negative behaviors and his own life experience. This will give you a better perspective when you are trying to understand the situation.

It is rare if not impossible that a person is all evil. Looking at it this way will help you become more objective and may even help you to feel compassion toward the person who caused harm either emotionally or physically towards you. This is not an excuse but an explanation. Excuses remove the element of responsibility but explanations create compassion.

3) Take responsibility for your part.

Taking responsibility is not accepting blame. I want to clarify that taking responsibility empowers you whereas blame is still pointing fingers and finding fault. That type of action disempowers you where as the former empowers you. Taking responsibility for yourself or a given situation means that you are not a victim, that you have a choice to learn from the lesson and move forward from it. So many people confuse these two words when in actuality, these two words belong on opposite sides of a spectrum. One brings on depression and moves you down the emotional scale, whereas the other raises self-esteem and facilitates healing.

For instance, when you are in blame, you are in a negative state. You are going to further create low self-esteem; you're going to feel badly about things. You're going to feel badly about what you've done, or what the other person has done. When you're in blame, you're plummeting your sense of self. You lose all sense of worth. If you continue to blame yourself, you will probably go into a state of depression.

On the other hand, when you take responsibility for something, whether or not it was your fault, you acknowledge that you are in a proactive, positive state. You are taking measures to correct whatever has been done. You have a choice. You are empowered. You are in a state of humility, openness and positivity. So, don't confuse the two. Don't sit and blame yourself if you've done something you know is wrong and don't blame other people for what they have done. It doesn't help you move forward.

4) Find the lesson in the situation

As I mentioned before, lessons are presented to you in order for you to grow from them to move onto the next stage of your life. What's the lesson that you needed to learn? Rather than finding fault and being a victim, what lesson can you learn from this so that you won't subconsciously repeat this lesson again?

Seeing my dad become so negative around money reminds me that it's not something I need to repeat for myself. I don't need to blame him for the hurt he has caused me around money, but I do need to take responsibility and further find the lesson that's presented to me so that I do not repeat it. Most people don't realize that lessons are only repeated when we don't learn from them for our own good. Remember that in every challenge there is an opportunity for growth inside. You can't get to the other side without learning so it's up to you to find the lesson in your past situations.

5) Let go

Letting go is a powerful step and is one of the last steps of completing the process. Some people often ask me, how do you let go? Or, they tell me that they have trouble letting go. Well, now that you understand the process on a deeper level, what you can do is actually detach from the story and step away from it.

It can be simply writing it all down and burning it and throwing away the memories. I had a client that was subconsciously hanging on still by keeping her ex-boyfriend's possessions. Even though she had already detached and forgiven this person, she was still hanging onto his stuff. Because everything carries energy, sometimes it's better to let go. More often than not, we create more damage trying to hold on so tight when we could just simply let go and trust. It could also be sitting there and visualizing the story float away with a balloon.

5) Do a Ho'oponopono exercise every day for the next 21 days.

Ho'oponopono is an ancient, Hawaiian healing modality that has to do with four simple phrases. These four simple phrases allow us to heal ourselves and to also heal our relationships with other people as well as heal our relationship with money. Think of this healing modality as a way for us to change our vibrational frequency and to let go of a lot of things that no longer serve us. Ho'oponopono helps so that we can become a vibrational match to the things we want in our lives. It's very simple. All you do is repeat the following short sentences:

"I'm sorry. Please forgive me.
Thank you. I love you."

When we say these four phrases and we do it consistently, we then begin to let go of the lower vibrations. These vibrations are no longer compatible with our energy field and we allow ourselves to then start to tap into higher states of awareness as well. Then as we let go, it's almost like those weights we have carried for a long time no longer weigh us down.

There is a legendary story of a man known as Dr. Ihaleakala Hew Len, who cured every patient in the criminally insane ward of Hawaii's State Hospital — without ever seeing a single patient.

Dr. Len set up an office within the hospital to review his patient's files. While he looked at these files, he felt himself getting angry and upset at what the prisoners had done. Being a spiritually advanced person, he knew that he had to clear himself of these thoughts, feelings and beliefs about the prisoners.

To do this, he worked on himself by saying these four statements over and over. After a very short period of time, the patients all healed. In addition, the staff who had been calling in sick or quit started to love coming to work. Eventually, they had to close this section of the hospital down because all the patients were cured.

He used the legendary Hawaiian healing and cleansing method Ho'oponopono to accomplish all of this. It is based on healing through loving oneself. Dr. Len repeated the words "I'm sorry. Please forgive me. Thank you. I love you." over and over again while reviewing each file individually.

It's an incredible true story.

Your money mindset:

Say this aloud: By forgiving those who have wronged me in the past, I am opening up pathways of abundance to flow into my life. I am no longer holding onto the negative charge that I have associated with money due to these people and circumstances that I have made a negative association with in the past. Instead, I choose to cut the chords of attachment I might have created and set myself free. I choose to forgive. I'm sorry. Please forgive me. Thank you. I love you.

chapter nine:

THE FIVE MONEY LANGUAGES

Find out where you are at, where you are going and build a plan to get there.

- Robert Kiyosaki

My partner and I are both not the greatest planners. Let's just say that if we had the choice, we would pay someone else to do all the planning for us – especially when it came to traveling. I'm the type of person who likes to see anything and everything on a given trip. My mantra is: "Not a day goes by wasted." On the other hand, my partner likes to relax in one spot. His mantra is, "Let's sit in one place and do nothing." Therefore, when we travel together, there's a lot of compromising that needs to be done.

On our trip to Costa Rica two years ago, I thought I'd try planning from scratch a shot. I began by spending an obsessive amount of time on Pinterest finding things that I thought the both of us would enjoy doing. I wanted to see sea turtles, visit every waterfall and go to the world's largest dog shelter. I then proceeded to make a list of all the things we would be doing as a result of my search.

Turns out, Costa Rica is pretty ginormous. The place we would go to see sea turtles was in a place called Tortuguero which is in the North Caribbean of Costa Rica. Meanwhile, where we were planning on staying was nowhere close to where I wanted to go and all the places I wanted to see.

Turns out, I didn't factor in where we were staying when I was planning our trip. I was just focused on all the things I wanted to accomplish and see.

Turns out, I'm not the only one that makes the mistake of undermining their current situation to get to where they want to go. A lot of people actually don't know where they currently are. At least not truly. In fact, a lot of people tend to start planning where they want to go, before knowing where they are at the moment.

Getting Crystal Clear on Finances

It's time to take a really good look at your current relationship with money and where it stands. If you're not 100% satisfied with the number in your bank account right now, it means that there's still work that needs to be done.

In this chapter we are going to get crystal clear on where you are RIGHT NOW when it comes to your finances.

Most people don't like to be in this position because it's uncomfortable. Rather, I want to encourage you to see things differently by seeing that by knowing exactly where you are right now with your finances, it's actually an empowering position. And that's because it will help you get super clear on exactly where you are currently and what needs to change moving forward.

A lot of people teach goal setting – meaning that in order for you to get to where you want to go, you are taught to write down all the things that you want to do or have or even become in the next few months, next quarter or by next year. That's the whole point of a vision board. In other words, it's called having a clear vision.

However, what most people forget is that before you can begin to plan the future and have a vision, it's important to acknowledge where you are at the moment. So many of us get caught up in the future because it brings us a sense of hope. It's really fun to plan the future, dream and visualize what's to come. But before we get to that part though, it's absolutely crucial and essential for us to understand where we currently are - especially when it comes to money.

Here's another example that might make sense to you.

I use to travel a lot when I was living in Armenia. In fact, I found a lot of value from traveling on my own and experiencing a new culture.

However, have you noticed that when planning a trip, especially when you are purchasing your plane tickets, when you are on Google flights, or Expedia, or Kayak or whatever airline platform you use to purchase your tickets, they always ask you, #1, where you want to go, meaning your destination, and then #2, where you are flying from aka where you are right now? Makes sense, right? How can you get to your destination if you are not familiar with where you are right now?

And for some reason, it makes sense when it comes to travel but so many of us don't use this concept to apply to our financial situation or when we want to create more abundance and wealth.

Instead, we dream up a good dream, or go straight into the visualizations and the manifestations. But it's important to understand EXACTLY, with extreme detail where you are right now.

Now I want to emphasize, knowing your current location or situation when it comes to money DOES NOT keep you stuck. This is the part where I feel a lot of my clients have resistance in. They resist looking at their current situation because they think that where they are right now defines who they will become. Where you are right now DOES NOT determine where you are going. This is just a way for you to get clear on how to make your next moves.

Sure, at the time being, it may seem painful and not at all fun, especially if you are buried in student loan or credit card debt. But when you really take the time to understand where you are, it actually empowers you to take the action steps to get to where you want to go.

In my case, I like to say it actually grounds me. Whenever I am working on a project and I start to feel uneasy or something may be wrong, I always stop and ask myself, where am I currently? How can I get more grounded because by doing so, the steps to move forward shows itself to me a lot easier and quicker.

Your Relationship with Money 

So, the first step to understanding where you are with money is to first understand that you are in a relationship with money.

Yes – a relationship.

Obviously, money is not a human being and we see it on a logical level as a piece of paper, but if it's just a piece of paper, why do we have so many feelings around money? Why does it make us feel a certain way and act a certain way? The answer is because at the end of the day, we have a relationship with money. Whether you like it or not, you have a relationship with money and this chapter is all about understanding your current relationship with money.

Now, when it comes to any type of relationship, I really believe that there are five key components that make up a healthy relationship: communication, respect, trust, acceptance/gratitude, and core values.

Think about your relationship with your best friend, partner, spouse, or even your parents. Wouldn't you agree that these are the five key components that create a healthy relationship? That's why I truly believe it's important for you to develop and improve on these components while you rebuild your relationship with money.

Even with my partner, we are always working on these five components in our relationship. How often are we communicating with one another? Do we respect each other? Am I trusting him when he tells me that he's hanging out with the guys on a Wednesday night?

Am I accepting of his qualities? Some relationships wish that their partner is a certain way, and they are hoping to change them to be the way they want them to be. But the truth is, my partner is the way he is, and instead of trying to change him, I must realize that I can't, and that the only person I can change is myself.

So, let's break down each of these five components in detail from a money perspective; I like to call it the five money love languages. While going through these five components, ask yourself if you've been practicing them thus far.

The Five Money Languages

1) Communication:

Money obviously can't talk back to you, but you're communicating with money all the time. For example, how frequently do you say negative things about money? How often are you saying that things are too expensive, or rich people are a certain way? How often are you watching movies and news that subconsciously affect the way you view money?

Let's use the example of your best friend again. Take a moment to close your eyes and bring about the face of a dear friend of yours. What if you were constantly gossiping behind her back, saying negative things about her; such as, she is stingy, or full of herself, etc.? Would you have a good relationship or bad relationship with her?

Communication can also be in the forms of frequency. How often are you checking your bank account? Do you often dread paying your bills or looking at your bank account?

Imagine, if you were dreading to see your best friend, or you choose to be inconsistent in texting or calling or even hanging out with her. Would you have a relationship with someone like that? Why would money want to be around you if you were constantly saying negative things about it?

Proper communication is crucial when it comes to your relationship with money! Be mindful of how your communication style is with money.

2) Respect:

The definition of respect is: *a feeling of deep admiration for someone or something elicited by their abilities, qualities, or achievements.* So, I want you to ask yourself, are you currently respecting your relationship with money or are you disrespecting it? Money within itself has the ability to give you things like food, electricity, WIFI, Amazon Prime, etc. Are you admiring this ability that money gives you or are you disrespecting money? Do you use and spend money without thinking about it, and abusing its power, or are you respectfully using it?

Everyone's relationship with money is different, so I want you to think about this carefully. Or, maybe you are hoarding money, and keeping it all to yourself. Is that respect? When you are in a relationship with a person, would you hoard all of your time with them? Or would you trust that when you let them go and let them do their own thing, they'll not only come back, but come back 10x happier?

3) Trust:

With respect usually comes trust – the feeling that you can

count on the other person and that the person will never deliberately try to harm you. Trust, in turn, develops through honesty, transparency and consistency. People in healthy relationships keep their word and always know where they stand with one another.

I use to do this thing where I'd get mad at my partner for hanging out with his friends (true story) because I wanted to hoard all my time with him. I was thinking from a scarcity point of view because I thought by doing that, I'd have more time with him. But what did that do? It drove my partner away. I didn't give him space nor did I respect his decisions.

Trust is having faith that things will work out regardless of how bad it may look at the moment. I don't know your exact money situation but perhaps you're in a tight spot with money right now and you aren't trusting that money will come to you. This type of mistrustful energy will not bring money to you. In fact, it is going to repel any type of abundance from you.

Remember that if you want more money and abundance, trust that it's already on its way to you, even when you don't physically see it. Do you trust your friend when he/she says she's going to do something? Or do you constantly question his/her motives? Do you have to physically see your friend in order to trust him/her? I want you to apply these same concepts to your relationship with money.

4) Acceptance/Gratitude:

Are you spending a majority of your time wanting more – dreaming of more, without accepting and being grateful for what you already have? There is absolutely nothing wrong with wanting more (in fact, that's the intention of this book – to teach you how to create and manifest more money). HOWEVER, what most people don't realize is that you get in life what you are grateful for.

The best example I can think of is gift giving. For instance, my love language is gifts. I love to give and receive gifts. However, if I give a gift to you and you aren't appreciative of it, the chances of me giving you another gift is slim to none. Why would I want to continue to give you gifts if you don't even appreciate it?

The Universe probably thinks the same way when you are constantly complaining about your lack of money. Be grateful for what you have and more will come to you. It's about appreciating what you already have so that you are on a vibration that tells the Universe that this is what you want more of. Everything is perception and when I was finally able to accept my partner for who he is, for example, he started to show up more of what I wanted out of him, if that makes sense.

But if I spent the majority of our relationship constantly complaining, saying things such as "I wish you were a certain way, or I wish you would buy me flowers, etc.", it creates resentment and the vibration of resentment doesn't give you more. In fact, that drives people away. Do you want to drive money away or attract more of it to you? Practice gratitude daily.

5) Values:

Finally, the last component is values. At the core of making money is what you are planning on doing with the money after you make it, right? Everyone's core value is different and it's important for you to understand what your core values are so that when you make more money, you are still grounded as to what your core values are.

For example, one person may use their money and buy luxury items, such as a Louis Vuitton bag, or a Mercedes or a nice condo. I want to emphasize that there is nothing wrong with that. Their core value may be of abundance and so their lifestyle reflects that. However, let's say my core value is freedom, and I choose to spend the money I make on vacations, personal assistants, or anything that gives me freedom.

Again, there is nothing wrong with that either. Money is used in different ways, but it must reflect your values. This is why it's important to understand what your core values are so that when you attract more money, you stay true to your values. That is also why having more money doesn't change you. Money is only an amplifier and amplifies the person that you are at your core.

If you are a bad person, when you have more money, you'll do terrible things with that money. If you are a good person, when you have more money, you'll do good things with it. Remember what your core values are and touch base on it if you've lost touch with it.

Now that we have defined and acknowledged where we are when it comes to our relationship with money, it's time to actually get into your money numbers!

Your Money Numbers

Clearly, we don't go around telling people our five love

languages with money, right? We don't go around telling people that we communicate well with money or that we respect money by letting it go, etc. The way we talk about money in this world is through numbers! So, it's important for us to understand on a logical level, where we are with money NOW.

That's why, you need to sit down with your bank account and get crystal clear on the numbers in there. Remember, these are JUST numbers; it's the meaning that we put behind these numbers that causes us pain and suffering. It's time for you to get situated with the money in your bank account so we can attract more of it!

I like to use the example of Kobe Bryant when he used to talk about re-watching the games that he plays so he can see what he did wrong in order to fix what he has to fix moving forward. When he's watching himself play, he's not taking anything personally. He was looking at himself from an objective point of view; kind of like a coach. So, when you are looking at your bank account, remember to put on the hat of a coach. Your emotions are not allowed in this playing field. It's all about looking at things from a bird's eye view and objectively making changes.

Again, most of us have an idea of where we are going. We have a vision of how much we desire to make, what life looks like at the next level, and what we would love to experience when we have more money. The problem is, most of us are blind to where we currently are. We have a rough idea, but don't know our exact location which prevents us from moving from where we currently are to where we want to go.

How to Get Crystal Clear on Your Money Situation

1) Do a self-audit of where you currently stand with money when it comes to the five money languages; communication, respect, trust, gratitude, and core values.

What I like to do is rate myself from 0-5. I ask myself: How often am I communicating, respecting, trusting, being grateful, and acting on my core values when it comes to money?

The reason why I do this is because when you can honestly rate yourself, you'll know exactly what you need to work on. Numbers are a great way to measure something. Remember, if you can't measure it, you can't manage it.

2) Look into your bank account and get clear on the number.

What I like to do is pull out a spreadsheet and keep myself organized. If I have any debt I owe, I write it down. If I have money coming in from different sources, I write it down. The purpose of this is to get crystal clear on where you are currently when it comes to your finances. The mistake that a lot of people make is not really knowing what is coming from where. If you don't have the specific detail amount, how can you expect more to come to you? Get detailed on where you are right now with that number that's staring right back at you.

3) Be mindful of where all your streams of income are coming from.

Again, this goes back to managing and measuring. It's empowering to know where everything is coming from.

4) Get clear on any money leaks that you might have.

Money leaks can come in the form of subscriptions that you have opted into and are paying for each month that you aren't using, or they can come from money that you owe or is owed to you that you need to take care of. It could even be that you own your own business and someone is trying to purchase something but they can't. If you aren't mindful of all the leaks and do something to fix them, money may be leaking away and you'll have no idea. The leaks may not matter in the time being, but over time, it can become a big issue. Be mindful and fix them now before the situation gets bigger than it has to.

5) While you are doing all of this, imagine that you have a coach's hat on, or physically put on a hat to remind yourself that your emotions are not involved in this process.

The reason why people invest in a coach and my clients invest in my services per say is because a coach can see things that they can't. We are emotional human beings. Sometimes, those emotions can fog or block us from seeing a decision or a picture clearly. What often gets in the way are our negative emotions. When we become too emotional, it fogs up our judgment. Therefore, when you are doing this exercise, it's important to remember that you are a coach looking at your situation. If you need to physically put on a hat and that act can help you remind yourself of the process, then by all means do that. Sometimes, physically doing an act can help you make the process a lot more enjoyable and easier.

Your money mindset:

Say this aloud: The more I understand that all money is, is energy; the more I can see that the way I treat money is how I would treat any sacred relationship close to me. Instead of fearing money, I can now see that by practicing the five money love languages, I can start fresh and build a strong relationship with money again. Getting crystal clear on where I am at now helps me pave the pathway of my financial abundance.

chapter ten:

THE GOLDEN RULE OF FINANCES

A bad day for your ego is a great day for your soul.

- Jillian Michaels

I was once surfing the web when I came across a picture of a horse tied to a blue chair. When I stopped the scroll to take a second look, I realized that the chair the horse was tied to was actually plastic and weighed no more than five pounds. It's the ones you can find at Walmart or Target for ten bucks.

It's cheap, it's lightweight, and it's a piece of fake, backyard furniture that a child can break if it really wants to.

I'm looking at this picture thinking to myself, "Wow, the horse has no idea that the chair weighs nothing and he can simply just escape with ease."

And then when I look at the text surrounding the picture it reads: ***"Sometimes the thing that is holding you back... is all in your head."***

I must admit, from an outsider's perspective, I can see how easy it is to just escape. After all, I'm the one that's on the outside looking in.

However, as I saved that picture in my favorites folder, I realized how we all fall victim to the biggest enemy that's standing in the way of us reaching our deepest desires, living the lifestyle that we want, and finally becoming the person we were meant to be. And **that enemy is *ourselves.***

I know, it's annoying. Trust me when I say that I have encountered myself many a time while I'm trying to climb this mountain that holds the treasures of my desires at the very top.

I've encountered her every time I lost focus and took a break.

She snuck up on me when I was on a roll making consistent 10k months and begrudgingly reminded me that I'm having way too much fun making money and life simply can't be this good.

Ego: Our Biggest Frenemy

Allow me to introduce to you our frenemy: Ego.

So why the frenemy? Why does it have to be that our Ego is both our friend and enemy?

Well for starters, our Ego is simply our protector. Back in the stone age when our ancestors were hunting for food, our Ego was there to remind us that when we came across a saber-toothed tiger during our hunt, it's our cue to run the opposite direction as fast as we can. In modern day times, our Ego shows up when we see the red light while we are driving a half a second too late, and we be slammin' on those brakes as hard as we possibly can. See how your Ego can be a great friend to you?

Without the Ego, we'd be dead which is why the Ego has been with us for so long. It's like that trusty mate you can turn to when emergencies happen. You'll know Ego will always have your back.

But no friend is ever perfect and here's where Ego has flaws. It only protects and sees everything as potentially dangerous.

That means that when you want to do something nice for yourself and commit to making more money than you can possibly imagine, your Ego will show up and remind you that if you fail, all hell breaks loose and the world is going to end. So, you don't go for the promotion. Or maybe you don't even start that online business.

Your Ego might be sitting right next to you asking you to stop reading this chapter because it's being exposed at this very moment.

Here's why it's essential for you to look over at your Ego right now and ask it to pack its bags and go on a vacation to Bali. For a month.

And that's because when it comes to rebuilding your relationship with money (so that you can attract and make more), your Ego can quite possibly get in the way of your growth.

What we are going to do next is recommit and to choose to create a better relationship with money. And part of that is choosing WHO you are going to BE moving forward.

Introducing: Your Higher Self

The person who was making the types of decisions and thinking the thoughts that led you to this point are no longer serving you. It's time for your Higher Self to step in.

You may be thinking to yourself, "Well who the heck is Higher Self?"

According to Roxane Burnett, "Your Higher Self is, in simple terms, the highest aspect of you that can be attained and held in the physical body. It is the part of you that knows, sees, and understands at the highest level possible, while the physical part of you still continues to move around in the third dimension. Anchoring the wisdom of the Higher Self into your physicality is very much a part of our human spiritual evolution and purpose."

Basically, to put it simply, your Higher Self wants you to become the best version of yourself – the one that's been put on this world to carry out a specific mission, and to be in a state of abundance at all times – aka, life is good.

Part of rebuilding our relationship with money is being very aware of our decisions and whether or not they are driven by our Higher Self, or our Ego.

The ego is normally driven by fear and lack. Whenever you look at your bank account and you get that feeling of despair and worry start to kick in, that's your Ego.

Worry, I will remind you, does not help you solve your financial problems. Taking action and solving problems helps you solve problems. But you can agree with me that taking action and solving problems in a state of despair and worry only gives you more of it. That is why when you catch yourself worrying, overthinking, complaining or living in a state of lack, it's a sign to call in your Higher Self.

We definitely don't want that type of energy when we are trying to rebuild our relationship with money. It isn't sexy, and it isn't attractive. So, it's time we shift from our ego to our Higher Self.

Before you completely start wanting to get rid of your ego, I just want to remind you that your ego serves a purpose. You can't completely eliminate the ego, but rather, you want to accept it and know that it will always be there.

A great analogy to describe ego is something I got from a book I read called "Big Magic." In this book the author describes ego like a baby in the backseat of your car.

So, imagine that you are taking a road trip with your baby (which in this case is the ego). You have the baby in the back seat and whenever you look at the rear-view mirror, you see the baby. However, while you are driving, the baby starts crying and distracting you while you drive. Obviously you aren't going to throw the baby out the window or leave it off the side of a highway, but if you are driving and you get immersed in the crying of the baby, you'll get distracted and crash and then both of you are dead.

However, if you can just keep your eyes on the road, accept that the baby is there and just allow it to still cry, but remind yourself that you are in control and you know better – you'll survive. The truth is, that you DO know better. You are the adult, and you have total and complete faith in where you are going. The baby in the car is just a baby, and its scared and fearful behavior is trying to stop you from getting to your destination.

As long as you remind yourself of this analogy, then you can always remind yourself that you are the adult and your higher self can handle the driving.

Ego vs. Higher Self

To help to clarify what the ego and what the higher self is, let's look at some things each would say about your current money situation:

MANTRAS YOUR HIGHEST SELF (AKA THE REAL YOU) WOULD SAY...

I am and always have enough.
I am the creator of my own reality and can create any amount I desire.
Anything is possible.
I am an eternal being.
I love changing and evolving to get to the next level of abundance.
Life is abundant.
There is always enough to go around.
We are all one.

MANTRAS YOUR EGO WOULD ATTACH ITSELF TO...

I don't have enough.
I have no control over my finances.
Everything bad happens to me.
My goals haven't come true in the past so why would they in the future?
I am nothing more than a temporary body on this planet and when I die, I'll be gone forever.
Change is scary and bad.
My life is hard, I mean just look at it!
I must work hard and fight for what I want because there is never enough to go around.
We are all separate.
I need to compete in order to get what I want.

If the latter seems like it's something you are all too familiar with, I want you to take a good look at your current situation. Is saying these things to yourself, really helping you get out of your current situation? Is it really helping you?

If it's not, then it's time to start rebuilding your relationship with money with your Higher Self. Here is how it's done:

1) Get clear on who's been making all the decisions:

An exercise that I like to do is print out all my bank and credit card statements and see how I have been purchasing or spending money from a fear-based, Ego perspective as opposed to my Higher Self. Once I get clear on my financial habits, I can then create a game plan to move forward from. Then I can really create from a space that serves me than one that is created from fear and lack.

Here's an example:

I recently purchased tickets to a four-day conference event to learn more about marketing and sales. If I were to ask myself if it was a higher-self purchase or an ego purchase, it would definitely be a Higher-Self-purchase. The reason being is that the intention of the conference is that I can learn and up-level so that I can better serve my clients and create an even better business, right? So, I would highlight that as my higher-self.

An ego purchase that I did recently was something as simple as buying a burger that I didn't really want but I bought it anyway because I wanted to fit in. The story goes that I was at this same conference, with a bunch of friends and they all wanted burgers. Deep down I didn't want a burger! I really wanted a salad but I bought the burger because I felt that if I didn't purchase the burger, I would be judged.

It could be simple as that!! So, remember, these are examples but to sum it up, when deciding between an EGO purchase and a Higher-Self purchase, think in terms of "am I buying this out of FEAR, or am I buying this because I FEEL GOOD and I genuinely want it?"

2) Treat money the way you want to be treated.

Remember what I said about having a healthy relationship with money in the previous chapter? Even though it may sound ridiculous to think that you are having a relationship with paper, remember that money is not paper. In fact, it's the belief and meaning behind what we call money that creates money. Therefore, part of having a healthy relationship with money is making sure you treat money the way you want to be treated.

Here's an exercise you can try out:

What I like to do to make it fun and exciting is actually have money dates with my finances. I set a date every week where I go into my finances and spend quality time with my money. Just think of a relationship with a friend. How often do you spend time with them? For me, I text my friends on a daily basis and I see them weekly. So, you can think of spending time with money the same way!

Remember, the way you treat money, is how money will treat you!

3) Remember, you are the co-creator of your financial reality:

If you are not happy with the amount of money in your bank account or how much is coming in each month, you have the ability to change it. Simply switching your perspective to a creator's mentality will allow you to see things from a different point of view. The next time you catch yourself saying horrible things about yourself, or money, remember that it's your ego trying to cause a ruckus. Once you realize that and have gained that awareness, it's simply just shifting those thoughts to be the opposite and reminding yourself that because you are the creator of your own reality, you can create your financial reality now.

Your money mindset:

Say this aloud: I'm aware now that whenever I feel bad about money, I am slipping into and making decisions from my Ego. In order to achieve maximum abundance, it's all about making decisions from my Higher-Self. I can always tap into my Higher-Self by seeing things from a higher level. I don't need to rely on fear to be the driver of my decisions. Instead, I can rely on my Highest-Self to make decisions out of love and light.

chapter eleven:

WHAT YOU SEE IS WHAT YOU GET

Create a vision of who you want to be, and then live into that picture as if it were already true.

- Arnold Schwarzenegger

I clearly remember my partner asking me when I first hit a $20,000 month as an entrepreneur, him asking, "Kristen, how do you feel???"

Thinking back, I don't recall feeling anything out of the ordinary! In fact, I remember not feeling anything, it kind of just felt normal.

"Really? You just feel normal? That's weird."

And the moment he said those words "That's weird," that's when I started to panic.

I had thoughts like, "Oh my God, I must be ungrateful for not feeling ecstatic for hitting my income goals." I started to feel guilty, and questioned myself, "Why do I just feel so normal" and I started to feel bad for wanting to feel something I wasn't feeling.

The truth was, I have visualized and lived out what it was like to make $20,000 months the year before. Up until that point, every single day, I have visualized with absolute clarity and have felt the feelings of what it was like to make $20,000 months every single day. In fact, I have even recorded myself a year before declaring that I would make $20,000 months and I have listened to that same recording every single night before I went to bed. Especially on days when I felt lost and defeated, I would whip out that same self-recording and play it as if it was a 10-minute guided meditation.

A year before I made my first $20,000 month as an entrepreneur, I was really struggling to make this whole online thing work. I felt like a complete hot mess and my belief in myself and my dreams were really low.

Being in this low vibration and this negative state of being wasn't helping me get to where I wanted to go obviously, so I started faithfully practicing visualization with clear intention every single day.

There's something about being at rock bottom that literally forces you to get back up and move forward because by that point, there's nothing to lose. And when you having nothing to lose, you have everything to gain.

Taking Visualization to the Next Level

What I did next was that I took it to another level. I spent an entire day in nature writing down all the goals that I wanted to accomplish, then I recorded myself reading this vision aloud and I would listen to it every single night while I drifted off to sleep.

Now I want to forewarn you, visualization is different than daydreaming. Visualization has intention and purpose behind it - while daydreaming is, well, daydreaming.

Naturally, I was an imaginative child growing up – my mind was always filled with random ideas. If you were to ask my parents, I was definitely the dreamer of the family. I fell into the habit of dreaming and imagining things in my mind but not painting a complete picture of it.

Visualization wasn't taught in schools during my time and even more so, in my parent's household, any type of imagination was looked upon as dangerous. Therefore, even though I had daydreams as a child, I quickly reminded myself to shut them off, afraid that my parents would see through me.

In my freshman year of college, I remember walking to class and having random daydreams and images of myself being interviewed by famous people. Even though those visions and daydreams felt warm and fuzzy, I always discounted them because I felt like it couldn't be realized. Basically, I never thought they would happen. After all, they were just daydreams.

So instead of painting an elaborate picture of it, I just allowed that dream to come in briefly and go out in a matter of minutes.

I never took my daydreams, ideas, and fantasies seriously until I was 27 and realized in order for me to truly become the person I wanted to be, it wasn't about 50 second random spurts of daydreams and ideas. I had to actually sit my butt down and write down and communicate in extreme detail what I imagined my life and business to look like. After I did that, I had to actually believe that my visualizations were truth. I think that is the #1 missing factor that most people miss. Visualization is not just bringing images and situations, and senses and colors in your mind. It's actually believing that whatever it is that you are seeing in your mind has ALREADY happened - that it is already accomplished.

Start Small

My advice is to really start small.

One of my favorite sayings of all time is to "learn how to walk before you start running." Even a toddler cannot run if they cannot walk first, so what makes you any different? Follow the cycle of nature of life instead of trying to resist and change it to be something that it's not.

Due to the overwhelming amount of information floating around in today's day and age, it's really easy for people to fall victim to this idea of microwavable results.

Remember that everything we see externally are highlight reels of everyone's life. We cannot take it at face value without considering the amount of work, focused dedication and discipline that was required for them to get to the level that you now see. The tip of the iceberg is not the whole iceberg.

So, when I say start small, I mean to start visualizing having amazing days.

Visualize in detail how your day will go. Start there. If that is too much for you, start visualizing a perfect hour.

Do you see how that's much more believable than trying to train your subconscious mind to believe that you're going to be interviewed by Oprah next week? Not to say it isn't possible, but remember that your subconscious mind isn't completely stupid. The real accomplishment you are trying to reach is believability over grand goals. The more your subconscious mind believes in what you are imagining, the more likely your goals will actually manifest into what you desire.

How Visualization Works

There was an Australian psychologist named Alan Richardson who conducted a now famous experiment in sports visualization and muscle memory. He gathered participants and had them shoot 100 basketball free throws, recording their base numbers.

He then randomly divided the participants into three separate groups. Group A was told to practice free throws for 20 minutes, 5 days a week for 4 weeks. Group B was ordered to do nothing basketball related for 4 weeks – not even to think of basketball. Similar to Group A, Group C was asked to come in 5 days a week for 20 minutes each but rather than shooting free throws, was told that they would be guided by a professional in *visualizing* shooting free throws without ever touching a ball.

After 4 weeks, Richardson had the subjects shoot 100 foul shots again. Group A had improved in their ability by 24%. Group B (the no-ball group) unsurprisingly made no significant improvement. Group C (the fantasy free throw group), however, improved by 23%, nearly as much as the group physically practicing every day.

Studies show that thoughts produce the same mental instructions as actions, and mental images impact many processes in the brain, such as attention, perception, motor control, planning, and memory. According to Lynne McTaggart, the author of *The Intention Experiment*, electromyography (EMG) has shown that the brain sees no difference between the thought of an action and a real action. When we perform an action, some specific neural pathways are being stimulated, and specific chemicals are being produced; the same physiological changes happen when we visualize ourselves performing that action.

Do you now see the power of visualization? Imagine

what could happen in a year if you practiced visualization every single day for a year. Before you go all crazy and start running, I urge you try it out for a week. Try it out as an experiment and see what happens!

Difference Between Visualization and Daydreaming

Remember when I told you growing up, I had a lot of daydreams? Well, many people mistakenly believe that daydreaming is the same thing as visualization, so they don't put much effort in it – and that's why they can't create a vivid image that feels real. As I previously explained, it has to look real to your mind in order to be effective. Daydreaming just happens, kind of like what I was experiencing during my daydreams of being interviewed by Oprah, for example. It's basically like letting your unconscious mind do whatever it wants. And daydreams are most often inconsistent – you don't usually daydream about the same things, playing the same scenario in your head.

However, when you add conscious action and intention into your daydream, it becomes closer to visualization. In other words, a visualization should have a firm structure and intention – it is constructed with the guidance of your conscious mind and needs you to fully concentrate and feel into it. Daydreaming rarely involves including other senses, and even when it happens, it happens by chance. Visualization is best when you're able to include all five senses to it, one by one, and to really see yourself in the image you've created.

Finally, day dreaming most often happens only in the

third person view and in future tense – you see yourself doing something, but it's from the outside. With visualization, the third person view is only one part of it that leads you to the first-person view, as if the visualized scene were unfolding all around you, and it happens in the present. It gives more power to the visualization and makes it real in your mind – whereas while you daydream, you know that it's a dream which is much closer to wishful thinking than to creating an environment that your brain will believe in.

That's why I'm a firm believer in not only practicing visualization on a daily basis so that it then becomes a subconscious habit, but also, I believe in listening to yourself talk about what you have already accomplished in detail.

Here's how I do it: I create something called a Painted Picture. I got the idea of creating a painted picture from Cameron Herold's book "Vivid Vision" and since made it my own and have taught my clients to do the same. I want you to take this exercise seriously because I promise you when you commit to it, you'll be able to reach your financial goals faster than you can possibly imagine. I have seen it work numerous times not only with myself, but with my personal clients.

How to Create a Personalized Guided Visualization

1) Find a place OUTSIDE of the office or your home office

Choose an environment that makes you feel at peace and where you'll be undisturbed. Personally, I love doing painted pictures when I'm on vacation or somewhere out in nature. Going to a nearby park would work as well. The reason why I personally don't create my visualization at home or at my desk is because I'm allowing my brain to be even more relaxed when it is surrounded by nature. There have even been studies that show that the *outdoors enhances your creativity* which is exactly what is needed in order for you to create a personalized guided visualization. Bring a notebook/journal and some water.

2) Get yourself into a meditative state.

You can do this by taking five minutes to yourself to be in the present moment and soak in your surroundings. While you are doing this, make sure you are sitting down while you are meditating. We don't want you falling asleep! The point of this step is for your brainwaves to be at theta/alpha state to increase relaxation and creativity. At this state, you can think creatively and really visualize. This step is all about priming yourself to start the visualization process.

3) This is when you start visualizing.

Start by thinking about your perfect day. Remember that it's okay to start small and work your way up. Imagine what your perfect day would look like. Perhaps you already had a perfect day in the past. Even better, bring that image up to mind and add anything you feel is necessary to make it an even better day. If you feel more advanced and have visualized before in the past and you feel comfortable thinking about your dreams in a span of a year, start the process of imagining a year from now, after you have reached your financial goals. Think of all the details and things you'll be doing and how you will be feeling. Get super specific because **the more specific you are, the better.**

4) While you are closing your eyes and visualizing, use one page of your journal and just start brain-dumping what you see.

It doesn't have to be full sentences; the point is just to write down what comes up. Feel free to brain dump as much as you want. You will see in further steps how this ties in together. Whatever pops in your mind while you visualize, write it all down. The great thing about this exercise is that it's personalized to you. No one else will have your exact dreams, goals, and aspirations. Remember to get crystal clear on what it is that you want.

5) While you are doing this, tap into your visualization more by adding in your five senses.

When you make the amount of money you desire, describe a moment of what you'll be doing. For example, let's say you are taking your parents out to celebrate – what restaurant is it? How do the chairs that you are sitting on feel? Visualize it down to the utensils. What's the smell of the food like? These details truly matter and that's how you get good at visualization and painting a very clear painted picture.

6) Again, remember to tap into your feelings.

This part is super important. Remember your subconscious mind can't tell the difference between something you vividly imagine, such as a goal, a hope or a dream—and a real experience! Feelings are the fastest way to actively visualize. Don't rush this process. Take as long as you need to really feel into the feelings of already having whatever it is that you want.

7) Pull out your journal

Start writing your personalized guided visualization in first person and in present tense as if it has already happened and how grateful you are for it.

For example: *I am now so happy and grateful that Mom, Dad and I tried Matsuhisa sushi for the first time to celebrate another successful month in business. Mom accidentally got wasabi on her jeans... etc.*

8) Finally, my favorite part: record!!

After you are finished with your entire painted picture, you are going to whip out your voice recorder on your phone. I use a voice recording app on my iPhone. Then you are going to read what you wrote with emotion and record it simultaneously.

9) Listen to your recording consistently

After you finish recording it, you are going to listen to it every single day before you go to bed! Or, when you wake up. Or both! Choose whichever way you feel motivates you more and that you are comfortable with. If you want, you can even add music to it. Now you have your own personalized visualization that's unique to you!

Your money mindset:

Say this aloud: Through visualization I am able to co-create the life I want and the money that will come into my bank account each day and month with ease. I understand that through repetition and an unwavering belief in my visions, I can literally create what it is that I desire. If experts, athletes and high performers can do it, so can I.

chapter twelve:

YOUR 'NIGHT KING' BELIEF

You don't become what you want,
you become what you believe.

- Oprah Winfrey

Growing up, I hated being Chinese. I think deep down it was because I had this deep-rooted belief that Chinese people were just not that important.

Here's why this belief rung so true to me; I grew up in the 90's and at that time there weren't a lot of Asian role models I could look up to. The only Asians I knew were my friend's parents who were doctors or worked at a corporate job like my dad. I didn't even know what a motivational speaker was. On top of that, what I watched growing up on television as a teenager was Topanga on *Boy Meets World*, and my favorite singer at the time, was Christina Aguilera. None of these women I looked up to as a child were of my skin color. Somewhere, somehow, I picked up the idea that Chinese people like me, did not matter.

If you look at childhood pictures of me, you'll always find me with a microphone or talking into the home phone. So, you can see that as a child, I have always enjoyed communicating with others and being in the spotlight. The truth was though, as I mentioned before, I had a deep-rooted belief that it was not possible for me, because I was Chinese.

My family also carried that belief as well. I wasn't encouraged to follow my dreams as a child. I couldn't dare say to my dad that I wanted to be a singer, writer or be on stages. Intuitively, that's what I felt happy doing, but to be quite honest, I didn't even know I could make money being a motivational speaker, let alone writer. In fact, I was consistently reminded to get good grades so I could get a good corporate job and make decent money. That was what was repeated to me day in and day out.

I remember this one time; I was singing "Beautiful" by Christina Aguilera in my bedroom and my dad started scolding me. Basically, he told me that I was wasting my time and I needed to hit the books. Singing was a waste of time he said. I remember feeling so ashamed and embarrassed and I started to believe that songs sung by white people were only meant for white people because words DID bring me down. Christina you were wrong!

I hated the skin I was born into so much so that I even changed my name to Noelle. One day in middle school,

I came home and asked my mom if I could change my last name to something other than Lee. She was unhappy and quite shocked that I would ask such a thing. She then said that I couldn't change my last name but I could change my middle name to Noelle. I saw on her face how my question must have hurt her feelings, so I agreed.

Fast forward after college days, when I was a Peace Corps Volunteer in Armenia, nobody believed that I was an American because all they could see was the color on my skin and the way I looked. I had Armenian guys follow me in their cars on my walk to work, and the whole time there, they would call me a liar and make fun of me for saying I was an American. Then it got worse because they would find me on Facebook and started spamming me.

That's actually when I decided to change my Facebook name to Kristen Noelle. And that's how the name Kristen Noelle came to stick.

I'm proud of who I am now, but it took many, many years of going through a lot of trauma and self-healing to be comfortable with who I am today.

Here's the good news. I truly believe that our experiences are placed into our lives for a reason, and it's up to us to reframe the stories and beliefs that we have developed over time that aren't serving us or holding us back.

For instance, even though I had a tough childhood, I can't blame my parents for any of it because they, just like me and you, are flawed humans. They taught me based off of what they knew from their parents. They were doing the best they could with what they had.

So, in order to move forward, it's important for us to reframe the beliefs that have become facts in our lives today because had I not reframed my beliefs three years ago, I wouldn't have written this book or become the person I am today.

Beliefs are much more possible than you may think they are. You may have a belief so engrained and subconscious that you don't even realize it's a belief.

Go Figure: Lesson from a Cockroach

The other day I was taking out the trash in my kitchen and I noticed that there was a dead cockroach lying on its back nearby my kitchen bin. My initial reaction was one of disgust. I got even more disgusted when I saw it moving its legs realizing that the cockroach wasn't really actually dead. Instead what it was really doing was trying to stand back upright and it was struggling to do so.

My partner just went out to pick up a few things at the store and was on his way back so I thought I'd wait until he got home to kill it. Yes, I'll admit I am a sissy when it comes to killing insects.

Moments later, my dog Manny comes over and starts to sniff the cockroach. I must have not caught the exact moment he did it because before I knew it, I saw the cockroach upright again and my dog just sniffing behind it. Basically, my dog helped that thing get off it's back and walking again!

I know what you're thinking – why am I reading this story and how does this have anything to do with me making money? Bear with me for one more second. You see, my beliefs about how disgusting cockroaches are to the point of desperately needing to kill it, are so strong that it's an immediate reaction of wanting to get rid of it. As a society, we believe that cockroaches are disgusting insects that need to be killed immediately.

Meanwhile, my dog has no belief whatsoever about the cockroach which allows him to have no attached emotion or feeling towards it. Immediately, I thought about leaders in the past who have killed so many people in the past without a flinch. Mass killings under communist regimes. What do you think people like Hitler or Stalin were thinking?

Beliefs can be so strong that people are killed with no reaction.

Why do we have such a different feeling when we see a moth compared to a butterfly?

Or a cockroach versus a ladybug?

We are able to reach out and touch a butterfly and allow it to land on us, but a cockroach? We would kill in an instant if we had the chance.

Money Beliefs Holding You Hostage

I really want you to think about how your money beliefs may be holding you hostage right now. After all, those beliefs have gotten you to where you are at this moment in time. Are these beliefs serving you? Or are these beliefs destroying you?

If you are not on the trajectory of living the life that you desire and find yourself stuck in a rut, then it's safe to say that your money beliefs are slowly killing you and it's time to adopt new beliefs. Here's a surefire way to be free of your beliefs:

1) Your thoughts become your beliefs which turn into your feelings and therefore gives you the green light to take action

You hear it all the time!

Take action! Implement. Get shit done!

The problem with taking action WITHOUT changing your beliefs first is like a hamster on a hamster wheel. You'll be running all your life and never getting anywhere. Or, maybe you'll get tired, come off the wheel for a week, wallow around, get back on the wheel and never get anywhere. Who wants that?

I was first introduced to the concept of thoughts, feelings, actions (TFA) when I first went to therapy. Basically, in Cognitive Behavorial Therapy you can change your results by first changing your thoughts/beliefs, which then changes your feelings, and then you'll take the appropriate action in order to achieve your desired results.

So, if you're not getting the results you want in life, especially when it comes to the money you want to make or the income you desire, your first choice of action isn't to find another strategy. That's the mistake I believe everyone makes at first.

Most people dive right into the doing part. "What can I do?" rather than focusing on what's even more powerful which is, "Who do I have to become?"

Here's another example:

Instead of asking yourself; "What do I have to do to make X amount of money this year?", you would ask yourself instead; "Who do I need to become and believe to make X amount of money this year?"

Here's another example:

Goal: Make $20,000 on my next launch

Thought: It's hard to make that amount in one go
Feeling: Scared, Afraid
Action: Not being able to show up powerfully and implement on all the steps.

Rather, here is what I would do to create a shift:

Thought: I've seen other people do it, so why can't I?
Feeling: Empowered, Motivated
Action: Showing up every day, doing what needs to be done and trusting the process

2) Be honest with where you are.

Can you see now why it's important for you to manage your beliefs and reframe them? Now, before we go into the process of reframing beliefs, I'd like to introduce you to something called the Thought Ladder.

Most people when they set goals, they set such big money goals that their subconscious mind just can't believe it and they end up not reaching their goals (not because their goals aren't obtainable) but it's because their subconscious mind doesn't truly believe it's possible for them.

So, in order for you to actually realize your goals, you have to do either of these two things:

#1 Lower your goals
or
#2 Adopt new goals that will help you get there.

Just think of it like a ladder, right? Let's say your income goal is $100,000 for example, and you have NEVER made that amount before or even close to it. You probably have to work on the beliefs that you may have in order to get you to your desired goal or you'll have to lower that amount so it seems doable to you.

Remember, you are a human being, it's absolutely possible to accomplish what you have in your mind but the path to getting there may take a little more time. Instead of trying to skip rungs on a ladder, try climbing each rung of the ladder first. It will get easier and easier over time, I promise!

3) Find the "Night King" belief and destroy it.

Typically, when we have negative thoughts about something, there's always one CORE deep rooted belief that is the MOTHER of all beliefs and negative thoughts. Killing this powerful, damaging belief will actually wipe out all the other beliefs in one go. If you watched *Game of Thrones*, you'll know what I mean.

The whole point of the last season was to kill the Night King because by doing so, all the white walkers would die simultaneously. However, if you were to just single handedly kill one white walker at a time, you'll tire yourself out and basically die. Your job is to find out what your "Night King" belief is and nip it in its butt. Basically, you're cutting off the head of a snake.

I got this idea from Tim Ferriss' book when he talked about the Lead Domino effect when it comes to productivity. He challenges people to ask each day, "which of these [tasks], if done, make the rest easier or irrelevant?"

I thought I'd apply it to our beliefs and thoughts and guess what? It works!

There's typically one CORE LEADING belief that when knocked down, all the other beliefs are irrelevant.

Which one is yours?

Mine was "Asian people are not important and therefore can't influence the world."

Remember, my beliefs were a story that I have created in my mind based off of what I saw as a child, it wasn't a fact. However, at the time I held it as fact. I grew up in a predominantly Asian community, no one was on TV at the time that was of my skin color and I was surrounded by Asians becoming doctors or lawyers, not motivational speakers, authors, or coaches.

So, how do we go about killing that one core belief? We question them by poking holes at the supportive evidence.

Here's what I mean:

Think about how this belief became so strong in the first place.

- I didn't see any Asians on television
- I didn't see any Asians as singers
- I didn't see any Asians in sports
- What I heard from my relatives and family members was that we shouldn't shine so bright. It was shameful to shine and we need to stay small and "humble" was basically what they said.
- "Don't gather so much attention" was what they said as well.

Think of all the reasons I gave above as supporting evidence to my one core belief. It's kind of like a tabletop supported by its legs, essentially. The reason why a table is so strong is because there are enough legs to support the table top. Once you start dismantling the legs, the tabletop can essentially break and fall down. Same goes with your beliefs.

It's time to kill your Night King aka CORE BELIEF that's sucking your life away.

4) Look for beliefs that come easy for you.

Change a belief that you have by comparing it with a belief that is actually serving you in your life or that comes easily to you.

For example, I had this belief that money is incredibly hard to make. So, what I did, was start asking myself, what comes easily in my life?

Well, making friends is super easy for me. I can literally make a new friend in the bathroom if I really want to.

Then I would ask myself, okay, why is it so easy for me to make new friends?

Well, the belief is that I'm an extrovert and that I enjoy being around others.

You see what I just did there? I identified myself to something that I wholeheartedly believed in. Whether or not I am an extrovert is irrelevant. Introverts can darn make friends in a bathroom too. But you see how the belief that you have has so much energetic charge behind it that it creates a very real experience?

You'll start to realize that something that comes easily to you was somehow programmed in the past that it was easy for you. Something happened in your past that formed the belief and now certain things are harder and/or easier for you.

Start stepping back and seeing that correlation in real life!

5) Question if your beliefs are really, actually true.

Most likely, your beliefs are not true. Yes, they may be true to you, but just because they are true to you doesn't necessarily mean they are true to me. If someone were to tell me five years ago that money is only energy, I wouldn't have believed them.

I believed that money was a struggle and I never questioned whether or not it was actually true. So, money was always a struggle. It wasn't until I actually questioned or probed at the belief that I realized that this belief that I carried around all this time was all in my mind.

Here's how you can question something's validity: You start looking for proof from other sources. I mentioned in chapter one that there are 1,700 new millionaires a day. Is that not proof enough that making money is getting easier by the day? If you are still resistant to what I just wrote down, is your belief still nagging at you to NOT believe what I have to say? Remember, when you can find supporting evidence to back up your beliefs, that belief becomes that much stronger.

All beliefs are created in our minds. What this means is that they can definitely be reframed and reprogrammed into better beliefs that could make you money. Start questioning and reframing those beliefs of yours that are holding you hostage.

Your money mindset:

Say this aloud: The actions I take or not take are all results of the beliefs I hold true in my mind. If I believe that money is hard to make, then it is hard to make. If I believe that money can flow effortlessly into my life, money will flow effortlessly into my life. It's time to go straight to the root of the problem by finding my 'Night King' belief and adopting a new money belief that actually serves me and the people around me.

chapter thirteen:

THE FORGOTTEN FREE TOOL

The words we choose can build communities, reunite loved ones and inspire others. They can be catalyst for change. However, our words also have the power to destroy and divide: they can start a war, reduce a lifelong relationship to a collection of memories or end a life.

- Simon Tan

"You spend $12.50 on five gallons of water a week?? Why?" That was the response one of my friends gave me when I told them about this place I get my water from called *A Divine H20.*

I have been getting water from *A Divine H20* for three

years now. A lot of people think I'm crazy because I spend 10x more than what most people spend on water, but honestly, I could care less because truthfully, I've never felt better.

I remember asking Sophie, the owner of the place, why some of the water in her store was more expensive than the others and what it means to have "Prosperity" labeled on certain types of water.

She then proceeded telling me about Dr. Masuru Emoto, a Japanese author and pseudoscientist who believes thoughts and vibrations have an effect on the molecular structure of water.

In his years of water research, through high speed photography of thousands of water crystals, Dr Emoto has shown the most beautiful crystals are those formed after the water is exposed to the words "love and gratitude."

He discovered that water from clear springs and water that has been exposed to loving words show brilliant, complex, and colorful snowflake patterns, while water from polluted sources or water exposed to negative thoughts form incomplete, asymmetrical patterns with dull colors.

Dr. Emoto conducted several experiments with his water theory, but my favorite one that I feel everyone needs to know about is his rice experiment.

Essentially what he did was place the same type of rice in three different jars and added water to each of them. For the first jar, every time he walked by it, he would say positive affirmations and kind words to it – words like "I love you," "thank you." For the second jar, every time he walked past it, he would say negative affirmations to it. "I hate you,

you are disgusting" was amongst some of the things he would say. Finally, with the third jar, he completely ignored it.

After a month, the first jar in which he spoke positive affirmations to, the rice gave off a beautiful aroma and it started to ferment on its own. The second jar which he said negative things to, started to rot. And finally, the third jar in which he ignored, turned completely black.

The fact that the human body is made up of 70% water can only mean one thing – the thoughts and the language we use to speak to ourselves can make a profound difference in our overall well-being and our ability to perform and reach our greatest desires.

I did some more research and discovered that infants are made up of 75% water! That is some crazy stuff. That basically means the words that we absorb as a child has a HUGE effect on how we view ourselves as we grow older.

Now I really want you to think of your everyday thoughts and what you choose to consume each day. Are they negative or positive? Would you agree with me that a majority of our thoughts are primarily negative instead of positive? What I've also realized is that we are our own worst critic and therefore, some of our negative self-talk can be so subconscious that it's causing much more damage than we anticipate it to be.

This is why it's so important that we become mindful of the thoughts and words that we say not only to others, but more importantly to ourselves!

Just like the air that we breathe is essential to our well-being which we often forget about or take for granted, the words that come out of our mouth can be looked at the same way.

Our thoughts and/or words are powerful tools that come free to us in the toolbox that was given to us when we came to this earth. Why are we taking for granted something that can make such a huge important difference in our day-to-day lives?

This is why I'm such a huge believer in speaking things into existence. Even the Bible has seven scriptures that emphasize the importance of speaking things into existence. Saying daily affirmations and mantras, for example, to oneself, is like Dr. Emoto saying his affirmations to water. The way you feel when you hear certain words affect your ability to perform and attract abundance. If you want to try it out for yourself, conduct your own experiment if you have to!

Stand in front of your bathroom mirror each morning after you brush your teeth and say "I am broke" to yourself every day for 30 days. Use a journal to track what feelings and emotions come up. Notice your ability to perform as well as show up. Are you performing better at work or not? How are your relationships with others as a result of your negative affirmation each morning? Track the slight changes that happen.

After that month is over, switch it up and instead of saying "I am broke," say, "I am abundant" and document the results that happen in the next 30 days.

How to speak things into existence in 5 minutes or less:

1) Express gratitude to the money already coming in.

The most potent tool that we can use is our ability to be grateful. It's something people underestimate, but when used on a daily basis, has profound rewards. If you are having trouble remembering to express gratitude, set reminders on your phone to remind yourself to do so.

2) Speak into existence the things that you want to happen but hasn't happened yet.

This is the best thing you can do for your subconscious mind. Because your subconscious mind can't tell the difference from what's real and what's not, you can hack your subconscious mind by saying things that hasn't happened but you want to happen. You can speak things into existence through the use of affirmations and one sentence mantras, or you can actually script it out. By scripting what I mean is journaling everything out and writing as if it has already happened.

3) Create personalized mantras that are unique to you and your given situation.

Here are two ways I create mantras that are unique, intentional, and personalized to me.

I basically ask myself these questions in order:

For example:

1. What am I wanting to achieve? (A 6-figure launch in my business.)
2. How am I going to make it happen? (By setting daily habits that gets me closer to my goal.)
3. Why is this important to me? (I want to aspire to be someone that walks her talk, not just talks her talk.)

MANTRA: I am committed to my 6-figure daily habits.

Here's another way to do it:

1. What disappointed me or didn't happen the way I wanted it to be? (I wanted more people in my most recent program.)
2. Why did it happen? (I got overwhelmed with my to do's and didn't manage my time accordingly to promote.)

MANTRA: I plan and organize my days in advance so that I can show up as my best self for my clients.

Now it's your turn! The reason why I like making personalized mantras is because sometimes when I just Google and find other people's mantras, they don't resonate with me and that's because it's their mantra and not mine. They came up with it, not me. I highly encourage you to create your own personalized mantras. You'll be more motivated to say them aloud each day to yourself because you'll have a personal connection with them.

I want you to use these two frameworks and create eight mantras from it. Once you create your eight mantras, print them out and put it on your vision board or somewhere near your office desk - some place where you'll see them every day.

Make it a habit to repeat these mantras OUT LOUD every single day!

I like to read these mantras out loud before I start my day, and sometimes I even do it twice or even three times a day. Let's say, for example, I'm speaking at an event and I feel nervous. I'll say them in the car or somewhere private.

And finally, the reason why I'm asking you to create eight mantras is because the #8 in numerology represents abundance and wealth. Remember, everything is intentional in what we create!

Your money mindset:

Say this aloud: "Words are powerful and can shape my reality. I have the ability to speak things into existence. Therefore, being careful of the things that come out of my mouth and thoughts that I think on a daily basis is essential to radically living the life I want and deserve. I have the ability and power to shift my financial reality using my words. From now on, I only speak words of financial empowerment to myself and others."

chapter fourteen:

WHAT GOES AROUND COMES AROUND

Only by giving are you able to receive more than you already have.

- Jim Rohn

I once donated $500 randomly to a Youtuber after watching one of her videos. I've never met her before, nor was I a subscriber of hers. I just felt called to donate $500 to her after watching one of her videos. As a matter of fact, I do this every month. I don't always donate to a Youtuber but I always leave aside money to give to another small business owner, entrepreneur or creator.

I use to be afraid of giving away money, so I'd donate

my time. My thought was that if I gave away money, that would mean there's less money for me because I had no idea where the money would then come from. But ironically, I'd freely give away my time because I knew that I would have more time.

Turns out, I had a pretty backwards mindset. If you think about it, money is something you can ALWAYS make, but time is something you can't ever get back. So, in actuality, time is actually more valuable than money. But of course, that wasn't my way of thinking during that time. All I believed was that money was sacred, hard to come by and I had to hold onto it for dear life.

Essentially, what was happening was that I was afraid of giving away money because I didn't believe that I had the capability to receive it the way I received time.

Again, it all comes down to your belief system which determines one's actions but what I find fascinating is that not only is it necessary to rewire our subconscious belief systems, it's also absolutely crucial that we give to receive.

Here's what I mean:

Take a moment and focus on your breathing. Start following your breath as you breathe in and out…INHALE… EXHALE…

Now, inhale again and hold your breath. Don't let go of it…How long can you hold your breath before you turn blue and can't help but exhale? I timed myself, I lasted about 45 seconds. Any longer than that, you'll start to feel like you're about to explode!

Eventually you'll have to exhale. To let go.

It works the other way around too. If you continue to exhale without taking another breath, you'll end up drained and gasping for air, completed exhausted. Breathing is a balance between inhaling and exhaling. One cannot exist without the other.

The same is true of giving. If you accept what is given to you without giving anything back then all you'll be doing is taking and taking until finally you are so burdened and overwhelmed that you will feel ready to burst.

Similarly, if you spend all your time and energy giving of yourself to others without learning how to accept what is given to you, then you will never be in a position to fully receive what the Universe has to offer you.

Giving back doesn't have to be about the dollars you spend – it is the effort that you put into the act of giving itself. Remember that all money is, is energy. Whether you help someone directly such as volunteering at a homeless shelter or giving to a charity or a cause you believe in, just remember that one cannot exist without the other. Giving is receiving and receiving is giving.

The most important thing to remember is that the act of giving back is all part of the process of receiving. It maintains balance in the same way that exhaling and inhaling allows when you breathe.

Have you been cutting the flow of abundance by not doing either of the two? Are you giving as much as you are receiving, or are you giving too much and don't know how to properly receive?

So, if you find yourself blocked in certain areas of your life or you are lacking in sufficient time, energy or financial resources, ask yourself:

Are you GIVING?
Are you giving of yourself? Your time? Your energy? Your resources?
Are you giving back with all your heart and mind in all areas of your life?

Because the old saying really is true…

IN ORDER TO RECEIVE, YOU HAVE TO GIVE!

Perhaps you feel like you've been giving yourself way too much and you feel exhausted. You feel tired of giving and want to receive more.

First of all, I'd begin by asking myself, am I properly receiving or have I been deflecting the abundance that's come my way.

For instance, I had a client that use to complain that she felt like she was always giving. She was giving to her children, to her partner, and to her clients. Giving, giving, giving. I then proceeded to give her a compliment by saying that I felt she was doing a really good job of being able to balance everything amidst the perceived chaos she had in her life.

It was as if she didn't even hear my compliment! She immediately brushed it off and changed the topic.

Does this sound like you? If so, how do you expect the Universe to give you more abundance in the form of more money when you can't even receive a compliment?

Perhaps you are just like my client, deflecting the abundance and hidden money opportunities that are already coming your way without even realizing it! Pay attention to what you are deflecting – you may be blocking your own ability to receive all this time!

So, practice inhaling AND exhaling, (giving AND receiving) and remind yourself of the balance between the two – that you cannot do one without the other and expect to thrive.

Realize that the art of giving exists within the very same balance that breathing does. They go hand in hand. The most important lesson to take away is to always stay open to receiving blessings from the Universe and make sure you remember to take the time to give and receive.

Why giving attracts more 

Even if you're currently broke with little to spare, just giving a tiny portion can have a powerful effect on your energy.

You'll feel good about yourself, and this in turn will raise your state of vibration, attracting more to come your way. The problem that most people have is that they want to wait until they have even more air before they exhale. You are always in a position to give. If you are not financially in a position to give, there are other means to give.

For money to flow naturally into your life you have to allow some of what you have to circulate. This is why giving attracts positive energy. Being afraid to spend any money at all suggests a lack and scarcity mentality.

You don't believe you have enough, and this belief in turn creates a cycle of lack, blocking the path for more money to flow in. Your job is to keep the pathways open and for things always to be in flow. Just like a blocked dam will cause problems, an energetic financial block will keep you from attracting more.

To wrap it all up in a pretty bow:

- Giving and receiving is like inhaling and exhaling; there is no way you can just do one without the other.
- If you can't receive small things like compliments don't expect to receive bigger things like money.
- Giving is one of the fastest ways to raise your vibration and to send a signal to the Universe that you are ready to receive.
- In order to receive you must give.

Your money mindset:

Say this aloud: I enjoy giving, as much as I enjoy receiving. I know that the more I give, the more I'll receive. Instead of deflecting what comes at me, I am willing to openly receive even if it may seem a little uncomfortable at first. I am committed to this cycle of give and take as much as a I am committed to my breath.

chapter fifteen:

BEFORE SHE SPEAKS HER HEELS BESPOKE

I always thought it was me against the world
and then one day I realized it's just me against me.

- Kendrik Lamar

I became a marketing consultant before I was even a marketing consultant. The year was 2013, and I just landed in Armenia with a hot pink Michael Kors luggage and three years of my early twenties packed into it. Whoever gave me the idea of joining the Peace Corps did a great job of persuading me because I'm sitting at the airport with a stack of Armenian study index cards in case someone tries to speak to me in Armenian ready to take on anything that was thrown my way.

If you were to meet me on the street, you'd never guess that I'd done something like the Peace Corps. In fact, Armenians in Armenia called me the girliest Peace Corps Volunteer; one that was not only well versed in fashion, but became a marketing consultant overnight.

To put it simply, here's what happened: They needed someone to help a group of eight women entrepreneurs with their marketing, they hand selected me because well, for no good reason other than that I was a capable human being that was just available at the time, and the next thing I knew, my job was to help eight entrepreneurs come up with a marketing strategy to sell their products.

Mind you, I never went to school for business or marketing. In fact, the closest thing to marketing was my journalism degree and even then, I honestly had no idea how I graduated with honors. The late-night cramming sessions before finals, downing 5-hour energy drinks at the library must have paid off super well. Worth every penny I tell you.

The point is, I became a marketing consultant overnight without any former education or experience and things turned out fine. In fact, things turned out MORE than just fine. Here's how I did it; I identified myself as a marketing consultant, started acting like a marketing consultant and got results like a marketing consultant. If you've seen *Catch Me If You Can*, my life was pretty much like Leonardo DiCaprio's character in the movie for three years – just a few steps ahead of everyone else in the organization.

The truth was, there were times in which I felt like a complete fraud and unworthy of calling myself a marketing consultant because let's face it, who am I (someone that in fact barely knows anything about marketing) to be helping people with their marketing. But then when I'm about five minutes away from booking a one-way ticket back home to California, something happens and I'm reminded by the women whom I'm serving, how much my help is actually needed. Like that one time a woman I know got beat up by her husband and she needed to make the extra money to take care of her kids.

When you are put in a situation where you witness such inhumane acts, you're not very concerned by your job title. In fact, that's the least of your worries, if you know what I mean.

Think about it... If moms could become moms without any experience beforehand, you best believe that you can become whoever you wanna be as long as you decide it to be true. Besides, who is ever truly ready to become a mom? Motherhood is like diving into the deep end side of the community pool, head first – you just learn as you go. The great thing is there are no managerial glass ceilings you need to break into – the first day on the job, you're called Mom whether you like it or not. Then you form your whole entire identity around the word Mom and you become one just like that. Easy peasy.

So why is there a huge gap between where you want to be and where you are now?

What's the difference between the Kristen who's making let's say $50,000 a year and $100,000 a year? or $200,000 a year?

Is it the things she has in her possessions? Or is it the person she has chosen to become?

Let me break it down for you in just one word: Identity.

Has it ever occurred to you that you can become whomever you want to become without having to wait? What is there to wait for? The real problem lies in the idea that you can't act like the person that is making the amount of money you desire simply because you haven't made the amount yet.

The secret is that there are no steps! The only thing stopping you is your mind.

The best example I can give you, is becoming a parent. The reason why you became a parent is because of a circumstance right? You get pregnant, your kid comes out of you and all of a sudden you have a new label to call yourself. But it's not like you have to take any tests, or go through any hoops to become one. In fact, when you become a parent, almost immediately it's like you know what to do, say and act. Did you have to go through many years of school to do so? Absolutely not.

The stories that you are telling yourself at the moment are reaffirming your identity. On top of that your current behaviors are simply a reflection of your current identity. What you do now is a mirror image of the type of person you believe that you are (either consciously or subconsciously). Want to become a millionaire? Are you identifying yourself as a millionaire, or are you waiting for yourself to become a millionaire before you started being like one?

The Recipe for an Identity Change

Changing your identity isn't nearly as hard as you might think. There are really just three steps.

1. Decide the type of person you want to be.
2. Prove it to yourself with small wins.
3. Rinse and repeat

First, decide who you want to be. This holds at any level—as an individual, as a team, as a community, as a nation. What do you want to stand for? What are your principles and values? Who do you wish to become?

Let's say you want to make money being a public speaker.

What would a public speaker do if public speaking is their full-time hustle? They'd speak. If public speaking was in your identity and this is your way of making money, you'd speak and you'd figure out a way to make money speaking.

The reason why you aren't living up to your desire right now at this moment is because you don't IDENTIFY with what it is that you desire. Stop trying to do more work. Start from the inside out. It's about BEING not DOING.

Here's the tricky part that a lot of people can't seem to get their minds wrapped around.

Being is a state, it's like being angry.

How would you expect me to ask you to do angry? It wouldn't make sense to you right? You're either angry or you're not, there is no in between.

Same goes with identity. Realize that you cannot explain a state nor can you do a state – you can only be a state.

So, you may think, okay, well something happened for

someone to become angry right? Let's say I'm driving on the highway and someone decides to cut me off. Because of that situation I can decide to become angry. Now notice what I did there, becoming angry is still a decision. Perhaps in another culture, cutting someone off may be a compliment. Do you see how everything that happens is due to the meaning you give it and then the rest follows?

Therefore, being wealthy, being happy, and being angry is all the same. It's a choice, and you can choose at this moment to become as wealthy as you want.

Here are three simple ways you can shift your identity to be aligned with money:

1) **Talk** like you would talk as if you are someone that makes the amount of money you desire.

2) **Act** like you would someone that makes the amount of money you desire.

3) **Embody** like you would someone that makes the amount of money you desire.

Your money mindset:

Say this aloud: Before I even open my mouth to speak, my essence and energy introduces me, therefore I am always living and being my highest vibrational self in all aspects of my life. I don't need anyone to give me permission or validation for me to be who I want to be. In any case, there are people out there less qualified than I am doing the things I want to do simply because they decided and committed to living out the person they wanted to be, not tomorrow, or next week, or even the next hour; they decided right now, and so can I. I am giving myself permission to live into the next level version of me right now.

Pillar Three:

YOUR FINANCIAL ENVIRONMENT

chapter sixteen:

HOW WELL DO YOU FENG SHUI?

Your environment is like a 3D vision board.
– **Marie Diamond**

In 2017, I was broke, living with my boyfriend and his brother in West Hollywood.

If you would have met me then, you wouldn't have recognized me because that Kristen was someone I wasn't very proud of. At the time, I had just quit my sales job because my then boss sexually harassed me and three of my coworkers in a hotel room during a work trip and I was going through a pretty tough time.

I was unfulfilled, purposeless, ashamed of myself and broke as a joke.

I remember having breakfast one morning looking at our living room and it suddenly dawned on me that I've been staring at a Clint Eastwood Dirty Harry poster for 183 days straight. I had a fully loaded pistol pointing at me every single day and I didn't even realize it.

On top of that, the walls were painted a shade of dark red. Looking back on it now, I have no idea what kind of mind space I was in to allow myself to subconsciously be surrounded by the color, bloody red and someone pointing a pistol at me every single day for 183 days. I get it though. When you are down in the pit, depressed and don't find meaning in your life like I was at that time of my life, you can't seem to see anything clearly.

Whatever I was eating that morning must have lit a fire under my behind because that was the day I went to the local hardware store, picked up two gallons of paint in the shade Sun Shower, primer, buckets, brushes and got to work.

That was also the day I said "Good riddance" and committed to closing that chapter in my life and started writing a new chapter – one that didn't include Clint Eastwood and his dirty pistol, a room full of bloody red paint, and a physical environment that no longer served the next level me I was stepping into.

As you can imagine, your home environment plays a rather large part in your overall well-being. And yes, when I mean well-being, I also mean your ability to make and attract money. In my case, I had a Clint Eastwood poster pointing his pistol at me when I sat and ate my avocado toast each morning. Unfortunately, our subconscious minds don't know the difference between a human size poster and a real life human. That's right; it doesn't know the difference.

Check this out: consciously, you DO know the difference but unfortunately our subconscious mind is the one that's really in control. After all, why do you think it's so hard for you to get the results you want? You really think it's your lack of will power? No, it's your over consumption of your limited beliefs that are really holding you back.

So, here's the thing, maybe you were like me, unaware of how your current physical home and office environment is affecting your ability to attract wealth and abundance into your life right now. Take a brief moment and look up from this page. Do a 360 turn if you have to, and really soak in the room that you're in right now. How do you feel? Be honest with yourself. Are you subconsciously downloading remnants of your environment that might be blocking you from receiving the amount of money you desire?

I know someone that changed the direction of his desk so that he started seeing and facing the door, put a globe on his desk, spun it every day and as a result doubled his income and started booking international speaking opportunities. You might know him as the author of the Chicken Soup for the Soul books Jack Canfield. In fact, he attests a large portion of his success to the energy of his home.

My Asian parents calls it Feng Shui. I like to call it energetic environmental design. You can call it whatever you'd like but the truth is, whatever you have going on in your physical space right now is going to energetically help you or energetically block you from receiving the good stuff. Remember when I said all money is, is energy and everything around you is energy? Yes, that means that the artwork hanging in your office space has an energetic charge to it. The book sitting on your desk that your friend let you borrow has an energetic charge to it. Everything has energy!

Even money! If you treat everything around you with respect, including the inanimate objects in your home, watch your life unfold in ways you wouldn't ever think possible.

If you believe an inanimate object carries no emotional energy, tell me what you did with anything a previous lover gave you when the relationship ended?

You drove to that sucker's home with a cardboard box and threw it on the front lawn, right? Why would you want to keep anything that reminds you of him/her? You know on some level that you'll still be connected to them. Unless that's what you want, then in that case, that's a different story.

Even Marie Kondo, organization expert and founder of KonMarie Media greets her clients' home before her consultations. What she does is find a good spot in their home based off of her feeling, sits on her knees and literally greets the home like it's a person. She claims that by doing so, the home has a part in the tidying process. If Marie Kondo can treat a space with respect, I want you to ask yourself if you've been doing the same with your physical space.

If you want to energetically re-design your home so it invites in more energy, abundance, and good juju, here are a few ways to start:

1) Start fresh and declutter your space:

Go through each room in your home, work office, or wherever you spend the most time at and dump everything in the middle of the room. Carefully go through each item and ask yourself if the item you are holding represents the version of you that you've stepped into reading this book. If you don't see yourself bringing it with you to next level of your life, throw it away. Remember that everything has an energetic charge to it. If you don't want to keep your ex's guitar he left behind because it reminds you too much of the toxic relationship you two were in, why would you keep anything that holds you back from becoming the person you are stepping into? Conduct a burning ritual if you must. Get rid of the old energy to bring in the new.

- Ditch anything that feels energetically heavy/stuck or that you don't truly need. If it no longer resonates or works, toss it and simplify.
- Throw away old papers and organize your workspace. Discard anything that creates self-doubt or has negative emotions associated with it. Instead, keep what makes you feel confident and inspired.

When in doubt, move it out.

2) Take care and follow through on unfinished projects:

Following through is great energy. When you don't follow through on something, you're basically leaving your energy scattered in unfinished business. Unconsciously, not following through or keeping projects open ended when it was time to end can hinder us. In fact, when you start any type of idea, project or relationship, you invest your energy and time into it. A bit of your energetic self is placed into it. So, it's time to formally close off projects so that you can cut the energy leak. Ask yourself, what do you need to finish? What loose ends were left untied? Finally, what needs closure?

3) Smudge your space, especially your doorways.

Smudging is an ancient art that is believed to have been practiced by Native Americans for centuries. It's the name given to the ceremonial, daily act of cleansing and purification which uses a selection of herbs, often sage or palo santo, which are bundled together with string to form a smudge stick before being ignited. The smoke that's emitted from the herb bundle is believed to cleanse negative energy and purify living spaces, as well as people and even objects like tools, furniture, and home decor.

Similar to one washing their hands before a meal, it helps to cleanse a person in an energetic bath of aromatic smoke. Cleanse your entire home with sage focusing on areas like your door ways. Reason being is because energy comes from the outside in. You want to cleanse that energy and renew it so that new opportunities come your way through those doors and windows in your space.

4) Bring life into your living spaces

Super simple: buy a money plant and place it an area that you'll be spending a lot of time in. A plant is a representation of your growth and it can symbolize new beginnings. Nourish and take care of it. My only recommendation is to not keep any plants in your bedroom. Your bedroom is a place of rest not activity.

5) Install a desk water fountain in your space 

Ever walk into a Chinese restaurant and see a fish tank or water fountain? That's because it's believed that flowing water symbolizes consistent cashflow. It's not a coincidence that so many rich and wealthy people like to live right by the ocean, or they own a large pool. As long as water is flowing in a non-threatening way it symbolizes good cashflow. This means a regular pay check and a regular monthly income. Want to double the wealth? When water accumulates it signifies wealth and pile up of assets. It could be a pile up of assets like your company, property or business.

6) Place artwork that supports your growth

Remember that whatever you see on a daily basis affects you on a subconscious and conscious level. So be mindful of the images, artwork, paintings, and objects that you choose to place in your space.

Your financial environment:

Your home is truly your sacred space and your personal 3D vision board. Since everything is made up of energy, it's important to align your home to the energy of money by making sure it's not only pleasing to your eyes. It's also important to make sure that there is room for energy to flow. And most importantly, that you feel calm and confident in your own space. Your external home space is a reflection of your internal space.

chapter seventeen:

YOUR RIDE OR DIES

If you look at the people in your circle and don't get inspired, then you don't have a circle, you have a cage.

- *Nipsey Hussle*

I can't drink alcohol for the life of me without turning bright red and breaking out into splotches of hives all over my body due to an enzyme that 30% of Asians don't possess in their bodies. Thinking back in 20-20 hindsight, I see this more so as a blessing than a curse because while everyone else in college was getting wasted and spending Friday nights at the local bar, I was salsa dancing and learning how to ballroom dance. My obsession was so real. I was probably dancing five to six nights a week in an attempt to perfect my spin.

In fact, I remember one night I was driving back to my apartment on the highway at 2 am in the morning and started seeing lights behind me. Then on loud speaker I was asked to pull over to the next freeway exit because I was dancing to Marc Anthony. The cop that pulled me over asked me to step out of my White Honda Civic to perform a breathalyzer test he suspected I was drunk driving. Apparently, I was swerving like a drunk driver on the freeway. Oops. When he realized what was causing the swerving and making me buzzy and high on life was Marc Anthony's song *Ahora Quien*, I was let go with a warning.

That was the day I realized that I have been 100% indoctrinated into the world of salsa. And not the salsa you dip your chips in.

For about three years of my early twenties, I completely immersed myself into everything and anything salsa. I started off dancing at dance studios and had probably five pairs of ballroom dancing shoes in my car to match every type of outfit. I went to every event, congress, and get together I was invited to. The friends that I chose to surround myself with were as obsessed with the culture as I was, if not more. In fact, the reason I was able to perfect my craft so much was because I wasn't afraid to go up to random people and learn from them. I shamelessly invited myself to dance with better dancers than I was, so they could show me things I was still not an expert at. If I walked down the street, you'd think I came out of my mother's womb a born salsera.

Your environment is more powerful than your desire. That's why it's easy to binge on Netflix instead of working on your business when your partner turns on the TV and you're in the same room as them. Ever been in a group setting and the majority vote wants to eat burgers but you're over here trying to eat a healthy salad? It's difficult. Most likely you'll cave. You might as well just stay at home, right?

What people don't realize is that as human beings, we are tribal by nature. We like to be amongst other humans. We are social creatures. That also means that back in the stone age, you would rarely see someone hunt on their own. We are intrinsically linked to our surroundings and we are the most adaptable creatures on planet earth.

This can be a good or bad thing. Because human beings are the most adaptable creatures, we have the ability to adapt into more of who we want to be or quite the opposite, become people we could barely recognize (and not in a good way).

In fact, the fastest way you can be fluent in another language is by immersing yourself and living in that country. This is something I am actually familiar with and have experience with. In 2018, I lived in Armenia for three years, and became fluent in Armenian. I lived with a non-English speaking family in a small village. In a matter of months, I was able to watch Armenian drama and understand what was going on.

Perhaps you have a strong desire to have a better life, make more money, and become the person you've always wanted to be. But if you are in the wrong environment, nothing will happen. Or worse, you'll be discouraged to do what you really want to do.

The wrong environment can corrupt your desire, your dreams, and it can also corrupt your life. That's also why it's so important to surround yourself with people who you want to become and that will support you through your success.

I use to think that friends are people who will stick with you through the bad times. What I realized was that what's even more difficult (that not a lot people can do) is having friends who will support you through your success – not only be comfortable with your success, but rise to the occasion and have your best interest at heart.

For the strength of the pack is the wolf, and the strength of the wolf is the pack.

Here are some ways to equip yourself with a tribe that will help you live out your financial dream:

1) Cut off your right hand if it causes you to stumble.

I'm not asking you to literally cut off your right hand of course! Rather, I'm using it as an analogy. Even the Bible states that if your right hand causes you to stumble then cut it off, "for it is more profitable for you that one of your members should perish than your whole body to be cast in hell." The reason being is that everything is interconnected, even if we appear separate. Who you choose to surround yourself with will have an effect on you unconsciously. Make a list of the people that are holding you back and start distancing yourself from them. This may sound harsh at first, but the truth is that it's going to be hard for you to climb a mountain with your own baggage already, let alone choosing to carry theirs on your way up. Just like decluttering your home, it's time to declutter your relationships.

2) Have an open and honest conversation with what it is that you want and need.

Let's say that it's not as easy for you to cut off someone because they are a family member or spouse. After all, acquaintances are a lot easier to let go of than people who have been with you all your life. This is the time to have those tough conversations and share with them where it is that you are trying to go and who you are trying to become. Lay down the new law and ask them to join you. Tim Ferris said in his book *The Four Hour Workweek*: A person's success in life can usually be measured by the number of uncomfortable conversations he or she is willing to have.

3) Find your tribe in person.

Let's say you want to get better at marketing your online business or you're trying to master public speaking. Don't be sitting at home on your behind waiting for opportunities and friends to appear from thin air. Search for groups that meet in person that will help you develop this new skill. There are so many groups out there. You can even start by going on a website called meetup.com or even using Yelp to find classes.

4) Find your tribe online

The number of online groups that gather together for a specific cause or purpose is well... A LOT. Now more than ever, people are migrating online and spending more hours in front of the screen than interacting with loved ones in person. Obviously, spend quality time with your loved ones as much as you can, but if we were to look at the bright side, the internet has connected people from all over the world together. People who have different interests and passions can all just jump on a conference call to achieve a common goal. Take advantage of what technology has to offer you in this new era that we are stepping into.

5) Give value to get value.

Looking to meet your next BFF online or in a group setting? Start by offering something of value before you decide to dump all of your questions onto new soil. When you're committed to providing value to people first to nurture the relationship and stay focused on their success, (because honestly, people care about themselves first and foremost) you'll have more people who want to hear from you and support you.

Your financial environment:

Are you choosing your squad intentionally? Or are you allowing yourself to be around people that don't inspire, aspire, or lift you up? It's time to get a new gang of friends if the current ones you have don't have the same mindset as you. Your people environment is as important as your home environment!

chapter eighteen:

LUXURY IS IN THE DETAIL

We don't always get what we want,
but we do get what we tolerate.

- *Tony Robbins*

In 1979 a large passenger jet with 257 people on board left New Zealand for a sightseeing flight to Antarctica and back. Unknown to the pilots, however, someone had modified the flight coordinates by a mere two degrees. This error placed the aircraft 28 miles (45 km) to the east of where the pilots assumed, they were. As they approached Antarctica, the pilots descended to a lower altitude to give the passengers a better look at the landscape. Although both were experienced pilots, neither had made this particular flight before, and they had no way of knowing that the incorrect coordinates had placed them directly in the path of Mount Erebus, an active volcano that rises from the frozen landscape to a height of more than 12,000 feet.

As the pilots flew onward, the white of the snow and ice covering the volcano blended with the white of the clouds above, making it appear as though they were flying over flat ground. By the time the instruments sounded the warning that the ground was rising fast toward them, it was too late. The airplane crashed into the side of the volcano, killing everyone on board.

It was a terrible tragedy brought on by a minor error—a matter of only two degrees.

Two degrees.

How often do we overlook two degrees or perhaps minor details in our day-to-day life? Let's say you're cooking pasta and it calls for 8 minutes for the pasta to boil. Do you think it would make a difference in taste if we drained the pasta at 5 minutes?

Let's use money for an example. If you were given a 20% raise, would that make you happier? Or if you got a 20% pay cut, that would upset you wouldn't it? However, most people don't consider the details when it comes to attracting money. Moreover, what I use to do that made a rather large difference in my manifestation of money is no longer tolerating the small details in my financial environment.

Here's what I mean. Ever consider that you may be tolerating scarcity in your life right now? I use to think that just by shifting my money mindset, working on my subconscious thoughts and beliefs, and even changing who I decided to spend the most time with, was enough. It wasn't until I realized that although on a larger scale, I was making a rather significant change, I was forgetting the tiny details that I was tolerating in my life when it came to scarcity.

Take essential oils for instance. I'm a huge fan of essential oils and I have been using them for a while. I also believe that essential oils, when placed in a diffuser in your home can invite in great energy and purify a given space.

In order to save money, I use to purchase essential oils from Amazon. And the only reason why I was buying essential oils from Amazon was strictly because of the mere fact that it was a few dollars cheaper. I didn't even like that particular brand of essential oils. In fact, there was another brand that I much preferred but because it was a few dollars more expensive, I thought to myself that I'd rather sacrifice my happiness and my level of abundance in order to save a few dollars. I get what you're thinking. Well a few dollars add up over time! Do you know what doesn't add up?

The sheer fact that one cannot be in contraction and expansion at the same exact time. It's like trying to be at two different places at the same time. In one moment, I was declaring to the Universe and everyone around me that I was abundant, that I had an abundant mindset, but meanwhile, I was struggling to spend an extra four dollars to purchase the brand of essential oils that I absolutely adore. It's like subconsciously telling yourself that although you may be abundant, not all of your actions align with your beliefs.

Luxury is in each detail.

If your details in your life are still reactions to scarcity, then you are still living in scarcity and you are still vibrating at the level of scarcity, something that money is not attracted to. So, take a look at the details in your life right now that you are tolerating. After all, we don't always get what we desire, but always get what we tolerate.

What we get in life exactly matches what we are willing to tolerate. Nothing more, and nothing less. Whatever we have in our life is what we tolerate ourselves to have. Wherever we are in life stems from where we tolerate ourselves to be. We think, we act, and we behave the way that we do because we give ourselves permission to do so.

Now, if we want more out of life, if we want to change in some way or another, or if we simply want to feel more fulfilled, then only we have the ability to do so. The resolution to do so is actually a lot easier than some might think. We just need to be willing to tolerate less of the things that don't benefit us in order to get more of the things that we want. In other words, raise your level of tolerance. Just like what I shared with you with your financial thermostat, raising your level of tolerance is becoming aware of what scarcity you are tolerating right now.

Ask yourself, how can you choose abundance even in the small things? Remember that the creation is truly inside the details.

Here are ways you can raise your level of tolerance to money:

1) Set money boundaries:

One area of our lives that we're not always great about setting boundaries with is our finances. It's easy to allow others to overstep financial boundaries because talking about money (or saying no to people who ask for it) can be uncomfortable. It can also be easy to ignore our own financial boundaries, and we end up making mistakes with our money that hurt our goals in the long run. On top of that, it's not just about money. Indirectly, when you don't set clear boundaries on your energy, aka, your time and money, you end up depleting yourself and feeling bitter and resentful. Remember that at the end of the day, you are the one that is allowing what people can or cannot do to you.

2) Fully accept compliments and help:

Think of the last compliment someone gave you. Have you fully accepted it, or did you quickly deflect and compliment the person right back that just gave you a compliment because you were afraid of appearing egotistical? If you can't accept something as small as a compliment (again details matter remember?) how can you expect for the Universe to give you bigger things, like a bigger paycheck? Learn to accept compliments by saying "thank you" without feeling the need to say something back, even if it may seem uncomfortable at first. Get comfortable with receiving small things and the big things will take care of itself.

3) Honor your decisions:

Being wishy washy with your decisions is basically sending out a clear signal that you aren't clear about what you want. If you yourself don't know what you want, how would the Universe know what it is that you want? And feeling guilty or uncertain after making a decision doesn't make it any better, in fact, what it's really saying is that you either don't trust yourself, or you don't trust in general. Either way, if you can't even honor your decisions, you are just tolerating more indecision, uncertainty and scarcity in your life.

4) Make self-care a priority:

Are you skipping yoga classes during a big project because you're afraid that it will cut into you precious money-making time? If practicing yoga is a sure-fire way to get you into a better vibe, you best believe that honoring yourself and putting yourself first, as a result, will attract the right financial opportunities your way. As someone who is a strong advocate of interconnectedness and a holistic way of being, having the mind, body, and spirit in mind, your inability to toss your self-care rituals aside will send money running in the other direction. Have you considered that perhaps, we've got it all backwards as a society and that we can actually rest first before we work and take action? Don't grind when you need to take a twenty-minute nap. Honor what your body needs and get yourself into a higher vibration this way.

Your financial environment:

Turns out every nut, cranny and detail you are currently tolerating is contributing to your ability to attract more abundance into your life. Remember that you can't be in contraction and expansion at the same time. You must choose. If you are in expansion, then make sure that every detail in your life screams expansion! Moving forward, take a look at the small things you are committing to, setting firm boundaries on, so that you are not tolerating, but rather, attracting effortlessly.

chapter nineteen:

DON'T BELIEVE THE HYPE

Propaganda does not deceive people,
it merely helps them to deceive themselves.

- Eric Hoffer

After living three years abroad in Armenia, I came back to California applying for jobs. I remember having lunch with my dad one day after getting off my email inbox, lining up interviews for the next week, as we headed off to one of his favorite Chinese restaurants – Happy Family Restuarant.

"I think you should start watching the news," my dad said suddenly. A little taken aback by such a random request, I couldn't help but question why he thought it was so necessary for me to all of a sudden start watching the news – something I never did my 24 years of existence since that moment of time.

"Don't you think it's important for employers to know that you are up to date with current events?"

Um no. Quite frankly, any current event that's important or will affect my well-being and the well-being of my loved ones I feel like I'll eventually find out about through word of mouth. And by that time, it's probably something serious for me to actually consider taking action on, like the coronavirus. Other than that, I don't think it's necessary for me to engage with news that will not only distract me but bring me down. Do I think it's healthy to spend an hour or two or even three reading up on negative news just so I have something to talk about with my employer?

No. Here are three top reasons why consuming news excessively is bad for your well-being and actually stops you from attracting the money you desire:

- **Negative news stories increase personal worry.**

We're overwhelmed with negative news stories daily – especially if you're someone who opens up CNN the moment you open your eyes. Conflicts, natural disasters and other upsetting events are routinely pushed to our news feeds on social media, in newspapers and through our electronic devices. Often times we feel anxious when we hear about distressing events and have empathy for those who are affected. But, did you know that negative news could aggravate our personal worries that are not even related to the content of the news story?

- **Repeated negative news stories make us feel unsafe.**

Journalists have admitted that negative headlines outperform positive headlines and there is concrete evidence that we are neurologically wired to focus on negative information. The media repeatedly serves negative news because its proven to attract more attention, making their ratings go higher. When we're surrounded with global, negative or dangerous information 24/7, it makes us assume that things are more dangerous than they are. There's even a name for it, it's called mean world syndrome!

- **Excessive consumption of news destroys your productivity.**

Unless you have a pomodoro timer set up right beside you every time you consume information, and have enough self-discipline to go back to whatever it was that you were doing that's actually productive, most likely you're being pulled into the rabbit hole of article after article and pretty soon you find yourself forgetting what it was that you were supposed to do. This even applies to social media and who you are choosing to follow on social media. In fact, social media is designed to grab your attention and hook you in.

Propaganda, aka "news stories" and even social media is literally distorting your *reality*. The intention of information and content should be so that people could manage their affairs in their community. You need information to know what the opportunities are and what the problems are.

However, news and propaganda actually does the opposite of that. Most news stories are fundamentally opposed to what we actually experience on a day-to-day basis. Our perspective on the world is actually being skewed unconsciously and we make our interpretations because of it. In other words, news only shows the exception to the rule, never the rule itself.

For instance:

- How often do we hear about how many people love their spouses? Yet we get bombarded with how many people are murdered or raped.
- We only hear about war, violence, bad deeds, but never about peace, love, and happiness.
- We overrate terrorism and airplane crashes; we underrate noise pollution and chronic stress.
- Ever notice that the media never writes about itself? We often put it on a pedestal and don't question how they are actually contributing to our collective consciousness of our world.

Almost all news is irrelevant and only elicits more fear within you. And we all know that fear is not the vibration that you want to be vibrating to attract more opportunities in your life. In fact, it's quite the opposite. Abundance is not attracted to fear. And unless you are going to actually do something positive about it, the news is merely for your entertainment purposes. We might as well stamp the motto *"If you don't benefit from it, you are the product being sold."* It is not just there to inform you; it is also there to conform you.

Would you rather be conformed to make a lot of money, serve the world at a higher level, and give back to the community?

Or

Would you rather be conformed to be a scared victim, being herded like a bunch of sheep?

Bad news is really everywhere if you want to immerse yourself in it! You hear something on the news and it sticks in your head. Or someone tells you they don't think you'll get the job you went after because you're not experienced enough. Messages about the bad economy can permeate your thoughts. Paying attention to negative news or input from other people triggers fear. All of this sets the Law of Attraction into negative action.
Thinking about negative situations attracts those situations to YOU.

Here's the thing; you can't change the overall economy but you can change your response to it. You can't make other people stop dwelling on bad news but you can stop yourself. In the midst of all the chaos in the world, I keep my own little world happy and faithful. You can too!

When you choose to create your own reality, negative news in the bigger picture of the world can't hurt you. You can CHOOSE to attract positives by keeping your thoughts positive.

Here are ways to stay in your lane so you're not conformed by negative news:

1) Watch goodnewsnetwork.org 

There's a website called goodnewsnetwork.org that is all good, positive news. The website, with its archive of 21,000 positive news stories from around the globe, confirms what people already know—that good news itself is not in short supply; the broadcasting of it is. Remember that what you consume on a daily basis will make up your reality. It's not that there are no good news stories; it's just not being broadcasted in traditional news media.

2) Use technology and website apps to help you combat negativity.

I personally use a Google Chrome extension called Newsfeed eradicator. This prevents me from going down the social media rabbit hole whenever I login to Facebook in order to respond to my clients in my group programs. It's super common for me to see an advertisement or someone's post that might lead me astray even for five minutes and breaks my level of focus that I was already in.

3) Walk away from negative discussions

Remember that you are not a tree and you can walk away from anything that doesn't serve you. Or you can learn how to strategically change the subject when people around you want to go down the negative path of self-victimization and gossip. It doesn't serve you; it doesn't serve others and it definitely does not put you in a state of abundance, so why even engage?

Your financial environment:

Turns out, propaganda is everywhere! You'll find it from the news you watch, the discussions you choose to have, the social media accounts you follow, to even the mail you receive. Are you mindful of what you are feeding your mind each day or are you unconsciously feeding it junk food? Be mindful of what you are consuming and remember that you always have a choice!

chapter twenty:

DAILY MONEY HUDDLE

You'll never change your life until you change something you do daily. The secret of your success is found in your daily routine.

- John C. Maxwell

When I used to work at my door-to-door sales job, we used to do daily team huddles at 8 am sharp every morning. I remember my first day on the job when I was initiated into this practice. I thought to myself, all of these people standing around, gathered around this circle I was in, were definitely drinking some sort of Kool-Aid because I've never seen anyone, let alone a group, so stoked and energized to knock on doors for the next eight hours.

We did this daily huddle, well daily. There was not a day on the job that we missed doing it. Even when we traveled for work, daily huddles were done wherever we were at. We did daily huddles at coffee shops, in parking lots, at the mall – anywhere. If you could think of a random place, we probably had a daily huddle there.

The ritual typically began with our manager calling roll (literally like in class). We had to shout out that we were there. Then he said something inspirational for the day, recounted yesterday's performance and we had to go around in a circle sharing what our intentions were for the day including how many sales we were aiming to hit, etc. Then we all put our hands in the middle of the circle and lifted it and said "juice." After all of us said that, we had to run to our cars and drive to our "sales territory." In a nutshell, that was how our daily huddle was conducted every single day.

It was incredibly awkward for me in the beginning. Literally every single time I put my hands in the center for the first week I was on the job, all I could think of was how embarrassing this would be if any of my friends were there to witness. After a month of conducting the ritual, I noticed how it drastically affected my mood, energy and work performance. I found myself looking forward to going to work, more focused on hitting my goals, and actually hitting goals at the end of the day. At first, I chalked it up to the matcha green tea I would occasionally get on my way to work. But even on days when I didn't drink tea, I still had the same amount of energy and motivation throughout the day.

That was when I realized how important rituals and daily habits are to the success of our day and our ability to attract abundance.

Law of Action

Just like the Law of Attraction, the Law of Action clearly states that aligned action must be employed in order for us to manifest things on earth. The Universal Law states that we must engage in actions that supports our thoughts, dreams, emotions and words. In order for abundance to materialize, you must do the things and perform the actions necessary to achieve what you are setting out to do. Unless you take actions that are aligned with your thoughts and dreams and proceed in an orderly fashion towards what you want to accomplish, there will be absolutely no foreseeable results.

After we change our money belief and create a new story that empowers and helps us reach our desires, now it's all about taking action. However, taking action isn't a one-time experience. In fact, while 90% of the world is incredibly focused on instant gratification, the wealthy are experts on delayed gratification. That's because success and true abundance is truly a long-term game.

Anything takes time for it to materialize. Think about trees that you see in the forest or even at your nearby park; it took many years for it to grow. Even more interesting is that of the Chinese bamboo. Like any plant, growth of the Chinese Bamboo Tree requires nurturing – water, fertile soil, sunshine.

In its first year, we see no visible signs of activity. In the second year, again, no growth above the soil. The third, the fourth, still nothing. Our patience is tested and we begin to wonder if our efforts (caring, water, etc.) will ever be rewarded. Finally, in the fifth year – behold, a miracle! Or so we think. We experience growth. The Chinese Bamboo Tree grows 80 feet in just six weeks!

Difference between habits vs. rituals.

So, how do we take action on a daily basis and aim to be a practitioner of delayed gratification through our actions? We can start practicing money rituals and habits. Here's why I prefer rituals over habits. Well you may be thinking:

"What's the difference between habits and rituals? Aren't they the same?"

Yes and no.

Here's the thing; habits have been around forever. In fact, most of our habits are subconscious. We perform habits unconsciously on a daily basis based off of what we have believed until this time. Most of our habits were taught to us by our environment such as our parents, teachers, or our friends around us. For instance, me brushing my teeth in the morning and evening is a result of my mom helping me brush since I was a little girl. That was a habit that I adopted over time. If you have a habit of turning on your television while you eat dinner, that's also a habit that was subconsciously formed. Now, you probably don't even think twice before turning on the television. It just happens without conscious thoughts. Essentially, it's important to have subconscious healthy and positive habits that support the desires that we have set forth for ourselves.

Intentional rituals are a series of habits compounded that are better and more efficient. I like to think of rituals as Habits 2.0. They are the improved and more efficient version of habits. Not only are rituals a series of habits, but they are often fun too and inspiring to take part in.

The beauty of rituals is that they can contain multiple

habits in one ritual. Why focus on one habit at a time when you can do multiple at once? You can drink water after you wake up, floss your teeth, stretch and look at your goals as part of your morning ritual for instance.

Consistently taking action is really easy when you have a proven step-by-step action plan in front of you. When you don't have a plan and you make one up on the fly each time you perform a habit, not only will you be inconsistent, but also, you'll also get inconsistent results. Again, you're relying too much on thinking and willpower to figure stuff out each time you do it. That's why rituals should be done intentionally with a clear objective and a clear reason why.

Having a daily ritual will reinforce the new money beliefs you created in pillar two. Here are some examples of daily rituals you can incorporate into your day:

1) Have a gratitude practice

This is something I can't rave enough about. Gratitude is the one emotion that sends the vibration that you already are in a state of abundance. It helps you take inventory of how abundant you already are. You can create your own gratitude mantra that you say to yourself the moment you wake up in the morning. Personally, for me, this is something I do right after I spray my face with essential oil water when I wake up in the morning.

Gratitude creates abundance.

Complaining creates poverty.

2) Find new pleasures

For all of the activities that caused you stress in the past, ask yourself how you can create a more enjoyable, pleasurable ritual from it. For instance, checking my email use to be a huge chore but it was something I needed to do. I created my own pleasurable ritual by pulling up binaural beats and asking what type of opportunity does each email present to me each time I opened it.

Your ritual can be unique to you and you don't have to follow anyone else if you don't want to. For instance, I don't personally check my emails every day. And because we live in a society that believes that instant gratification is the norm, I set up an automatic email process that sends out an email immediately, if someone were to send me an email. The email states that it normally takes me 24 –48 hours before I can respond.

Fall in love with the journey as much as the destination. It's the details of the journey that creates your outcome.

3) Be present as much as possible

Stop worrying about things that haven't happened yet. There's a 99% chance that it's not going to happen. Worry is just a prayer for disaster. Start living in the now.

4) Visualizations, affirmations, and mantras

Practice your vivid vision or daily meditation and tap into that state of consciousness as if what you've asked for has already happened. I've said this many times in previous chapters, but your subconscious doesn't know the difference between what's real or not.

5) Track your results

What you measure will move. What you do not measure will not move. Track your rituals. Remember that you can't manage what you don't measure. Just like it's important for you to know how much money comes in and out of your bank account each month or each week, it's equally important to track your progress. That way, when you conduct a yearly review, you'll know exactly what you worked on. I like to use habit trackers to keep me focused on the ritual I'm trying to create.

6) Money Date – Celebrate the exchange of money.

Spending money, paying your bills, and receiving money should ALL feel good. In fact, it's something to celebrate. Yes, even when you are paying for bills. Think of it as just an indication that you have the money to pay for bills. Create a ritual every time you go through your finances. Light some candles. Celebrate any type of unexpected checks or deposits that come in. Put on your favorite music and make it a great experience.

7) Practice living the life you already want as if you already have it.

Who says you can't create a ritual of living the life you want as if you already have it? For instance, I have a friend who dreams of living in a specific neighborhood. She conducts a daily ritual of driving to that specific neighborhood, parking her car and walking around the neighborhood as if she lives there. So yes, definitely, drive through nice neighborhoods, practice experimenting and practice feeling abundant on a daily basis. I used to feel very uncomfortable going into higher end shops and that was because I felt as if I didn't belong there. However, deep down, that type of abundance was exactly what I wanted, so I had to practice getting used to that feeling. So, I started routinely going into higher end stores as a reminder that I can afford the things that I truly want.

Your financial environment:

Check this out: the actions you choose to take on a daily basis makes up the big picture. Setting up positive money rituals will not only intensify and help you manifest more wealth and abundance faster; it will literally set you up for success. Remember, anything that is done intentionally has more focused energy than just coasting through your work. Take some time to create money rituals that serve you and that put you in alignment!

chapter twenty-one:

THIS IS HOW TAO'S DO IT

Everything that happens, happens at the only possible time it can happen, and it is always at exactly the right time.

- *Wu Wei, I Ching Wisdom*

I almost cut my middle finger off one time making avocado toast for lunch and ended up in the ER with blood all over my shirt. I still remember the day super clearly; I had just finished wrapping up a call with a client and I had about fifteen minutes for lunch before I had another call at 12:15pm. Feeling super stressed and anxious, I tried to make my lunch as fast as possible so that I could go about my day. That particular avocado pit must have been super slippery because the next thing I knew, I lost control of my knife and I found myself lying on the floor of my kitchen with a third of my middle finger sliced open. I was rushed to the ER, had to spend the night at the hospital to conduct surgery the next morning because apparently, I had cut off the nerves in my finger. Till this day, I can't feel my left middle finger as much as the others.

I ended up having to wear a hand cast for four months which essentially forced me to slow down. (Try typing with one hand; it sucks.) Prior to this accident, the word "slow" did not exist in my vocabulary. In fact, I must have been born with the spirit of a hare because the thought of slowing down means that I'm put at a disadvantage, but more importantly, that meant that I couldn't be a workaholic. Cue the boos.

For an entire month, I resisted the idea of having to slow down. I didn't even want to entertain the fact that I could only work with one hand. I thought to myself, I must work harder during this time, aka, burning the midnight oil. I refused to surrender to the Universe slapping me across the face (in this case it was an avocado) to send me a very clear message to REST – thinking that through sheer motivation, grit, and willpower, I could be superwoman, do the imaginable and work double the hours.

Thankfully, every situation that happens in your life is meant to teach you something (although it didn't feel like it at the time) and through that experience, I've learned what it meant to surrender, trust, and let go. Once I was able to learn that lesson, I realized how much I was actually forcing myself to make money as opposed to allowing money to flow to me.

Are you flowing upstream or downstream?

First of all, I want to gently remind you of what money is;

it's currency. Money is supposed to flow. It's like water; it's a flow resource. Water crosses every boundary and territory in the world much like the way money does.

Just like money, water regenerates and cleans itself by moving. Also, water loses potency and stagnates when it is dammed up or still. Water and money are very similar.

And just like how water moves between people and hydrates us all, money follows the same principle.

If we buy $100 worth of goods, the $100 we pay for it then passes to the seller.

Then, that seller ALSO buys $100 worth of goods, giving it to a new seller who ALSO buys $100 worth of goods. All of a sudden, the $100 has bought $200 worth of goods, then $300, then $400…

Money isn't something that divides us, but something that holds us together.

Like the flow of water, we depend on to survive, money can't be stopped by any artificial barriers – and it shouldn't be, because it becomes unhealthy and stagnant. Money that is hoarded in the hands of people who don't live with purpose can destroy us all.

Because, just like water, we can drown in it – or we can die of thirst.

Now, think about how you have been making or attracting money into your life. Are you struggling and forcing it to come your way, or are you tuning into what you feel is aligned with you and then going along with the flow of the current? Most of the time, as complex human beings, we are so hardwired to see a project come through the way we want it to. Or, we think that the only way to make or attract money is through a specific opportunity which can cause us to lose sight of what the Universe is trying to show us – a pathway of least resistance.

Are we making things a lot harder than they need to be? How can we look at things differently to see how we can flow downstream instead of trying to force things to be exactly what we want?

Take my avocado accident as an example. At that time of my life, I was forcing myself to take on more private clients thinking that was the only way I could make money. I wasn't open to other ways of income or allowing money to come to me because I was so busy thinking that I was right. I could literally see an image of myself paddling like crazy against the current.

The moment I had my accident and was forced to slow down, I was able to take a step back and see that there were other ways I could make money and it didn't have to come with this one source I was stubborn to achieving. The moment I surrendered, the boat turned around and I started to ride the current downstream. No more fighting, no more kicking and screaming.

I like to think of all of this like the Taoist principle of Wu Wei. Wu Wei or 無為, translates from Chinese pinyin to mean "no-action" or "actionless action." This is considered the "natural" way to do things, as opposed to striving, pushing, and forcing. Before you shoot me a confused look and argue that action needs to be taken in order for things to be done, what I'm trying to explain is that Wu Wei doesn't teach you to not do anything, staying idle, or succumbing to inertia. Rather, it's about taking ALIGNED action, because when you love what you do, it doesn't feel like work. Therefore, in other words, you aren't really "working" if you don't feel like you are. Stay with me.

Think about the last time you were forced to do something. Did it feel good? Or did it feel yucky? As a result of being forced to do something, did you feel like your work was the way you liked it to be? That's why whenever I catch myself forcing myself to do anything, usually symptoms come in forms of panic, anxiety or overwhelm. At times like that I take a step back and ask myself if this is something I really want to do, or if I'm just doing it because everyone else is.

Here are a few ways to go with the flow, surrender and practice Wu Wei like the Taos do:

1) Remind yourself that life is a matter of balance, like the Yin & Yang symbol we so often see

Most people think of Yin and Yang like opposites. Rather, I like to look at Yin and Yang as necessities. One cannot exist without the other in order for us to appreciate the beauty in our lives. For instance, if the sun never sets and it's always available, we wouldn't appreciate the moon and the need for rest and recovery. It's absolutely necessary for one to go through challenging times and instead of RESISTING it like many of us do (aka try to get out of it by paddling upstream) we can allow these challenging times to wash through us and help us grow.

2) Play Mindball with yourself often

There's a game called Mindball (A game of competitive relaxation) that has been installed in several science museums in which two opponents are sitting on opposite ends of a long table and the goal of the game is to move the ball that starts off in the center to your opponent's side of the table in order to win. However, there is no physical action; instead, all the action is in the mind. Quite the contrary of trying hard to win, the winner is actually the person who is most relaxed.

You wear these headbands that track your alpha and delta brainwaves. The stronger they are (aka, the more relaxed you are) that's when you win. Too often, we are making decisions out of angst, or frustration, or out of anxiety. Next time, instead of making decisions with that type of energy, scale back and sit with yourself in silence and tap into your state of calm before taking any action or making a decision.

3) Ask for a blessing in the morning.

Part of my morning routine involves me asking for a blessing from The Universe. I recognize that although I can take 100% responsibility for my life, I can also allow some space for it to be unknown. I don't have control over every detail and it allows for me to trust that the Universe has my back. If I were to design every aspect of my life, it leaves no room for creativity, surprises and synchronicities to happen.

4) Surrender to the outcome

Ah – Surrender. This is the word that most of my clients hate whenever I bring it up during our client sessions. That's because all of us are so conditioned to do, do, do. Instead of trying to control, force, and make things happen surrendering means allowing things to fall into place once you've done all you could in a situation.

Trust that things will come to you when they come. The Universe has heard you once; you don't have to keep checking in to see if your wish has been fulfilled. In fact, don't be like the farmer who planted his seeds in the fields and every couple days, dug up the holes to see why they haven't grown yet. Once you plant your seeds and set your wheels in motion, give it time to manifest and sprout.

Your financial environment:

Surrender to the unseen, uncontrollable force that is much greater than you and me. Have faith that things will work out exactly the way they are meant to. The Universe has heard your desires and is currently materializing what it is that you want. Patience is a virtue.

chapter twenty-two:

FOLLOW YOUR BUTTERFLIES

Yesterday they called it coincidence.
Today it's synchronicity. Tomorrow they'll call it skill.

- Antero Alli

Not too long ago, I attended a meditation workshop in Los Angeles. The meditation class was titled: *Signs from The Universe.* In Chinese, we call it evidential occurrences, it's basically when you find encouragement from the Universe through signs in your environment.

To be honest, in the beginning of the class, I was quite irritated by the instructor. Call me judge-y but she came into class super flustered, out of breath and couldn't take her eyes off of her cell phone. Immediately I went into a judgmental state of discomfort, and I started to question whether or not I was in the right place.

She then proceeded to tell the class that the Universe doesn't speak in English; it gives us nudges through animals, symbols, and numbers. I'm sitting there thinking to myself, I know all of this, why am I still here? This went on for the next forty-five minutes, in which everything that came out of her mouth, I reacted with some sort of internal frustration. I couldn't pinpoint exactly why I was feeling the way I was feeling but all I knew was that I was uncomfortable and not at all happy.

Towards the end of class, I had an intuitive gut feeling to ask the Universe for a sign. Since my signs appear in the form of butterflies, I specifically asked for butterflies and a lesson that I needed to learn from this experience. Then, I reluctantly thanked her for the class and stepped outside. While waiting for my partner to use the bathroom, I decided to browse around the arrangement of jewelry they had in the waiting area.

Suddenly in the corner of my eye, I saw an intricate necklace with tiny butterflies attached to it. Immediately I went to reach for it shocked that my answer came so fast to me. Right when I reached for the necklace, I noticed a small sign right above it with a mirror. The sign read: "We are all mirrors of each other. What you see in others, exists in you."

The truth is, you are and will always be divinely guided. In my case, I needed to have a wakeup call that my frustration towards that particular meditation teacher was merely a reflection of what I was frustrated in myself. My judgment of her was my own judgement of myself. That afternoon, she was placed very intentionally in my path to remind me what it was, and that I still needed to work on it. We are all students of life. Luckily, the lessons that are presented to us at every stage in our life and even down to our day-to-day life are there to guide us. It's really up to us if we are willing to accept the signs presented to us.

I'd like to close off by reminding you that you too, are always divinely guided. The Universe is always sending you signs and synchronicities designed uniquely for you, to lead you to your greatest potential. Your job, is to merely pay attention to them.

If it's okay with you, I'd like to continue this journey with you. Remember those butterflies I asked you to keep track of throughout the book? I want you to continue to carry those with you.

From now on, every time you see a butterfly, take a moment and feel what it's like to already have the amount of wealth and abundance you'd like in your life. I want you to start being on the lookout for your own butterflies. They could come in the form of a drawing, something you came across online, or even a real butterfly. Every time you see a butterfly, feel what it's like to already be living and attracting the wealth and abundance you desire.

Remember, the purpose or intention is not to catch the butterflies and hold them captive, but rather, allow them to come and go as they please, trusting that you will see another butterfly soon.

The world desperately needs your presence, essence and gifts now more than ever.

I hope this book gave you the tools you need to stop chasing and to start attracting. Remember that you are already abundant, already wealthy, and already the person you desire to be.

Kristen Noelle

P.S. My love language is gifts. I hope it's okay that I've created another gift for you on the next page.

NOW'S THE TIME TO
KEEP THE MOMENTUM GOING!

Free Masterclass!

Discover How To Eliminate Your Top Money Blocks That Keeps You Staying Stuck, Self-Sabotaging and Under-Charging Using My 3 Step Propriety Framework

Watch this **FREE MASTERCLASS & HYPNOSIS SESSION** now, and say "YES" to becoming an energetic match to wealth and abundance!

https://kristennoelle.co/wealthmasterclass

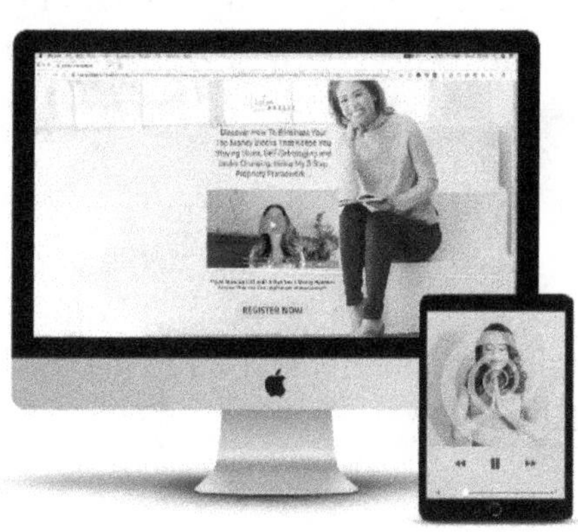

ACKNOWLEDGEMENTS

I am so incredibly grateful because it really took a village to help me finish this book and bring it to life! Steve Daughtery, my editor for encouraging me to keep going and combing through every detail of the book to make it as perfect as possible. Thank you for your attention to detail and making my words come to life. Sloane Ketcham, my literary mentor, personal cheerleader and book coach. I'd be lost throughout this process without your guidance and continuous support. Chandler Bolt and the Self-Publishing School team, thank you for creating such an inspirational container making the book writing process enjoyable and streamlined for me. Eric Van Der Hope, guiding me through production and going above and beyond to help a fellow author. My formatter, Juliet Nermal, for taking care of the interior design. My assistant Krizzel Aquino for holding things down while I had my blinders on wrapping up the book. My partner Roger Mansourian, without you I wouldn't have been able to finish this book at its entirety. Thank you for your ongoing support, pep talks, and lending me your shoulder when I needed it most.

Finally, I'd like to thank you, my reader for supporting me in my life's work by reading this book and sharing it with your loved ones. It really is because of you that I do what I do. I hope that this book gives you the tools to stop chasing and start attracting.

ABOUT THE AUTHOR

Kristen Noelle is an award-winning, transformational mindset and business coach, speaker, and entrepreneur, who helps small business owners, entrepreneurs and side-hustlers release their money blocks so that they can effortlessly quantum leap into the next level of their life and business. She has helped hundreds of her clients double their income in a matter of months, using her propriety 3 pillar method the Cash Flow Trinity™.

Kristen is also a certified Business and Feng Shui Consultant and has an extensive background in both marketing and Chinese metaphysics. Kristen's deepest mission is to help all visionaries step into their soul's purpose so that they can make the income and impact they were placed here to make.

To learn more about Kristen visit her website at http://kristennoelle.co

WANT INSTANT KARMA?

Thank You For Reading My Book!
I really appreciate all of your feedback, and I love hearing what you have to say. I need your input to make the next version of this book and my future books better. Please leave me a helpful review on Amazon letting me know what you thought of the book. Thanks so much!!

~ *Kristen Noelle*

CPSIA information can be obtained
at www.ICGtesting.com
Printed in the USA
BVHW071527100721
611576BV00003B/387